I0478908

USA
Coloring Book

Adult Colouring Books

Aryla Publishing 2018

978 1 912675 02 9

www.arylapublishing.com

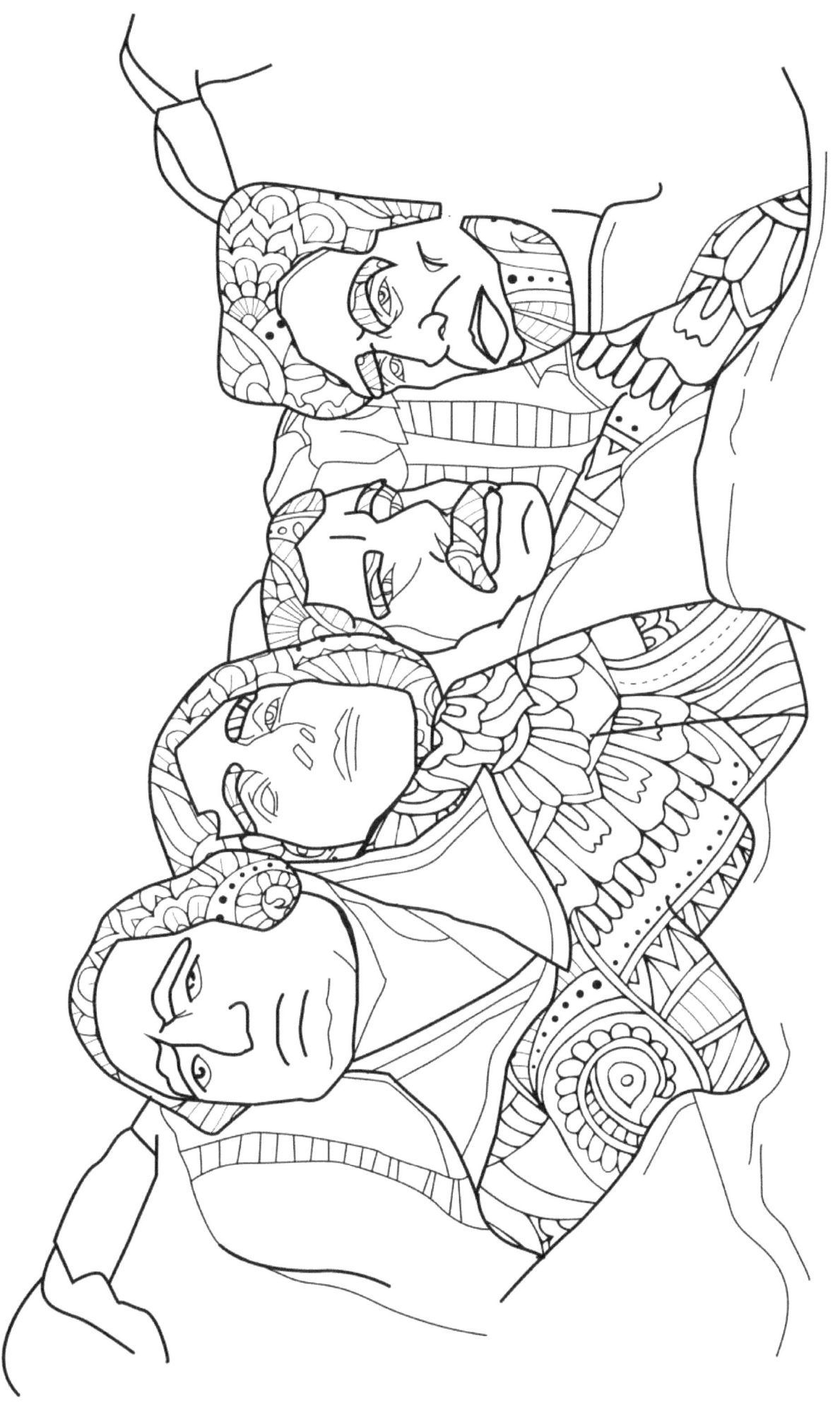

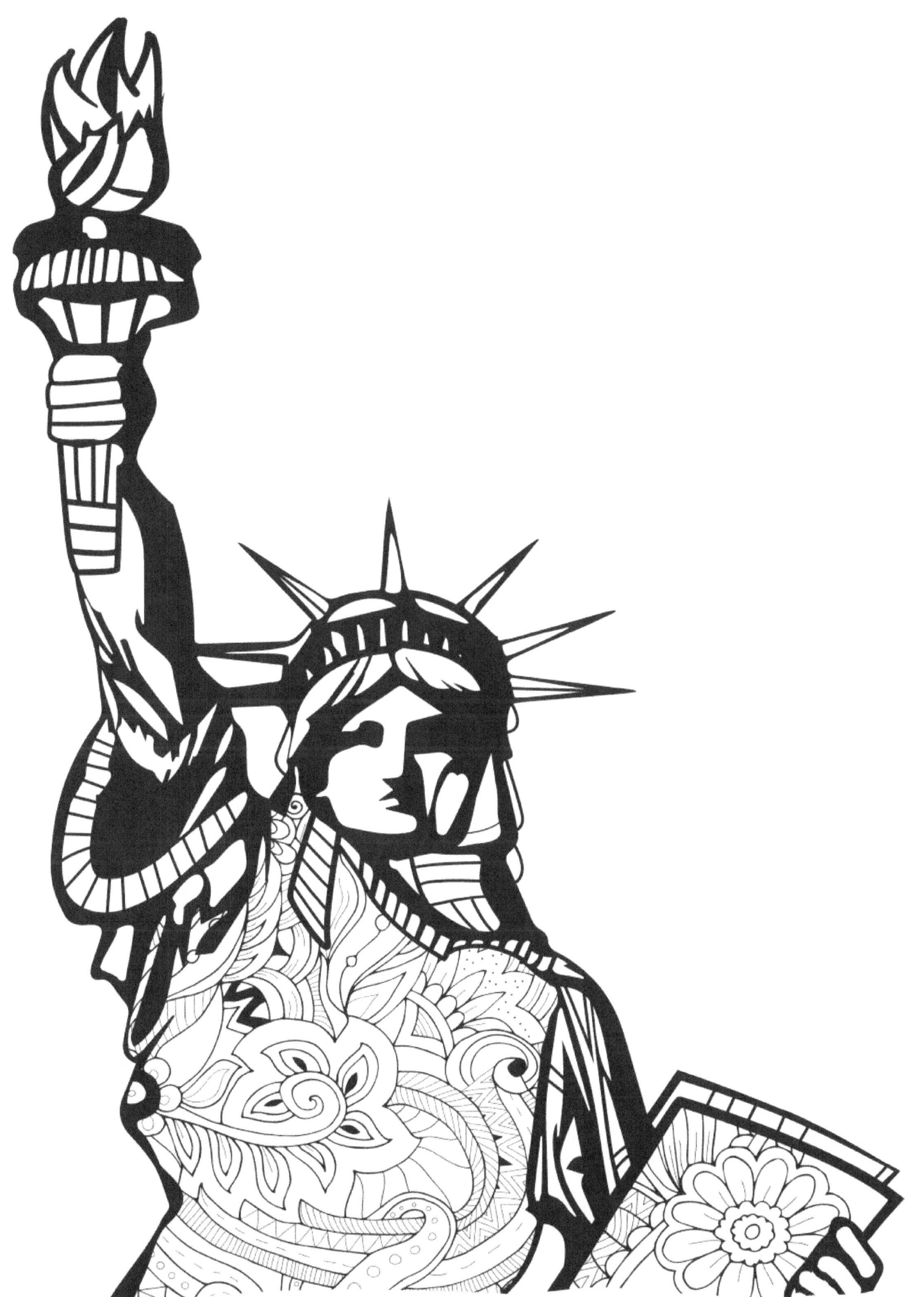

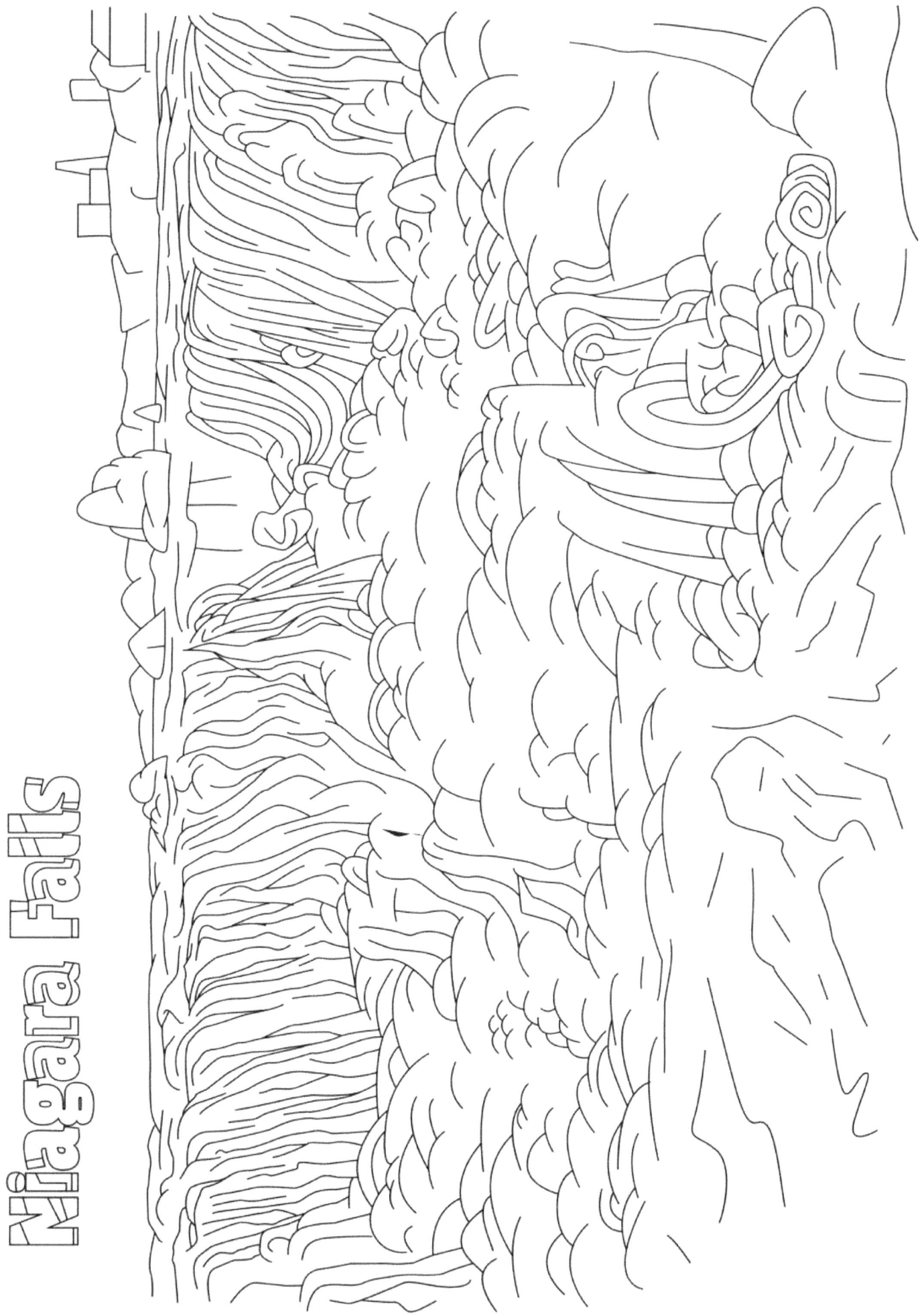

Niagara Falls

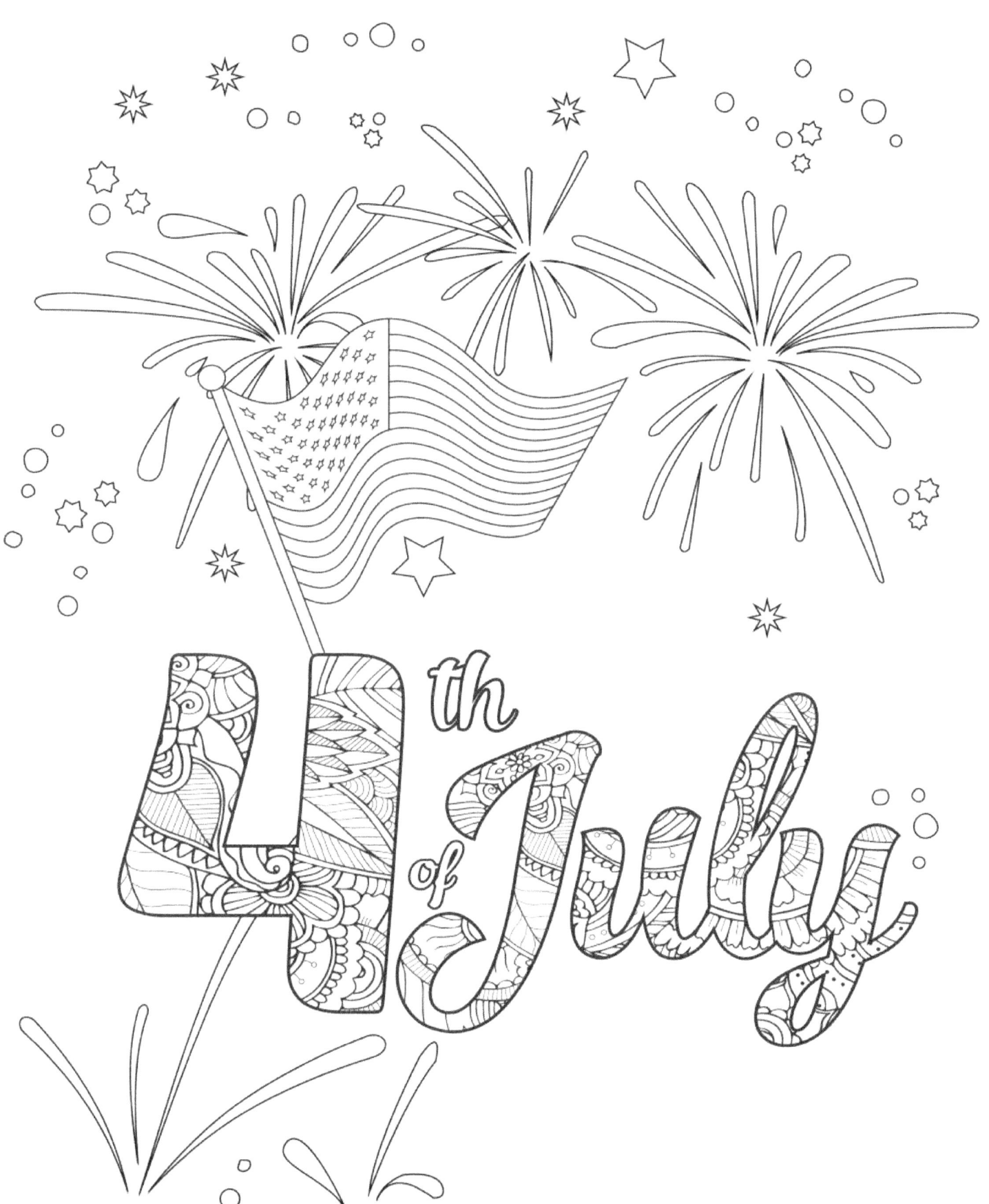

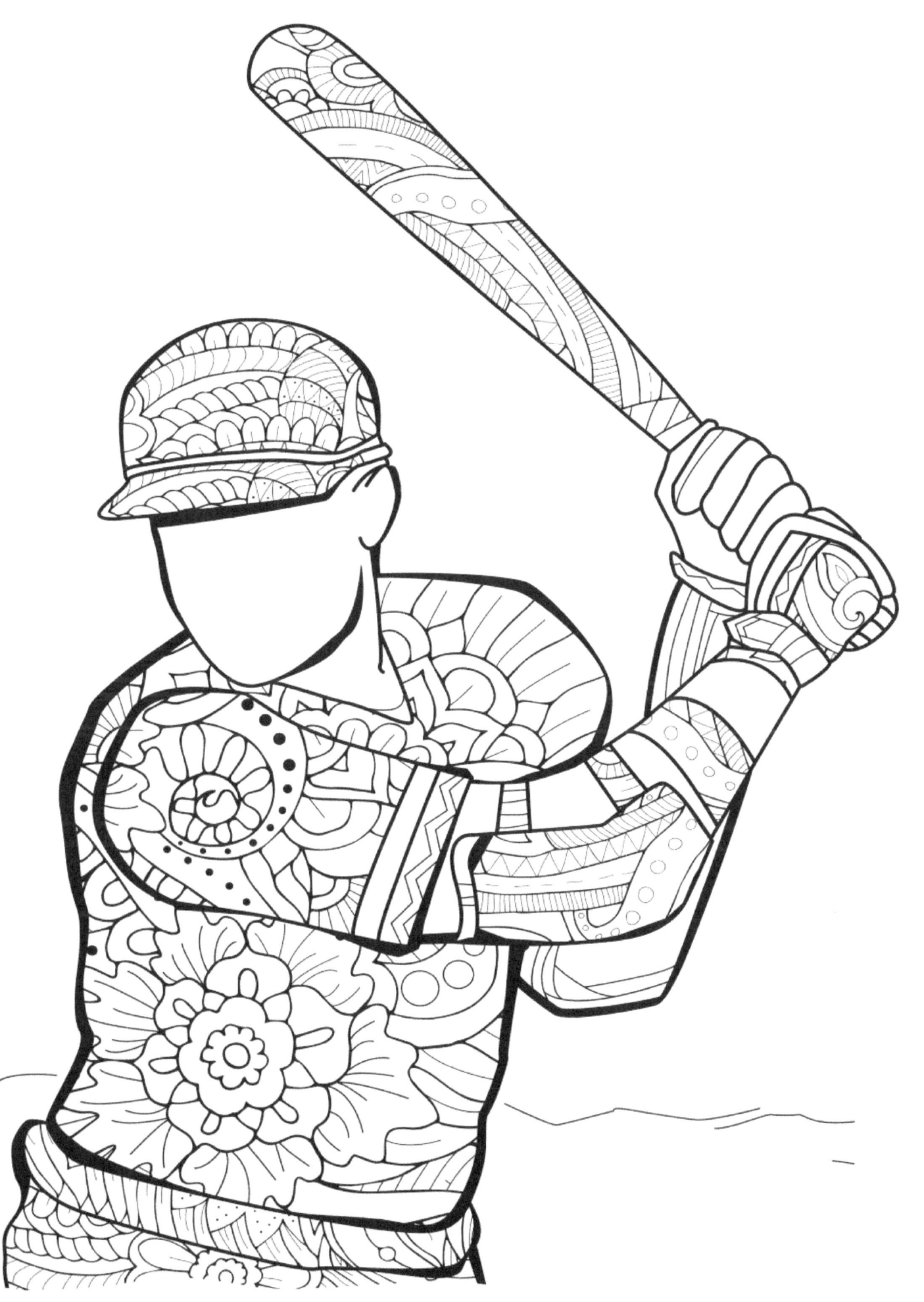

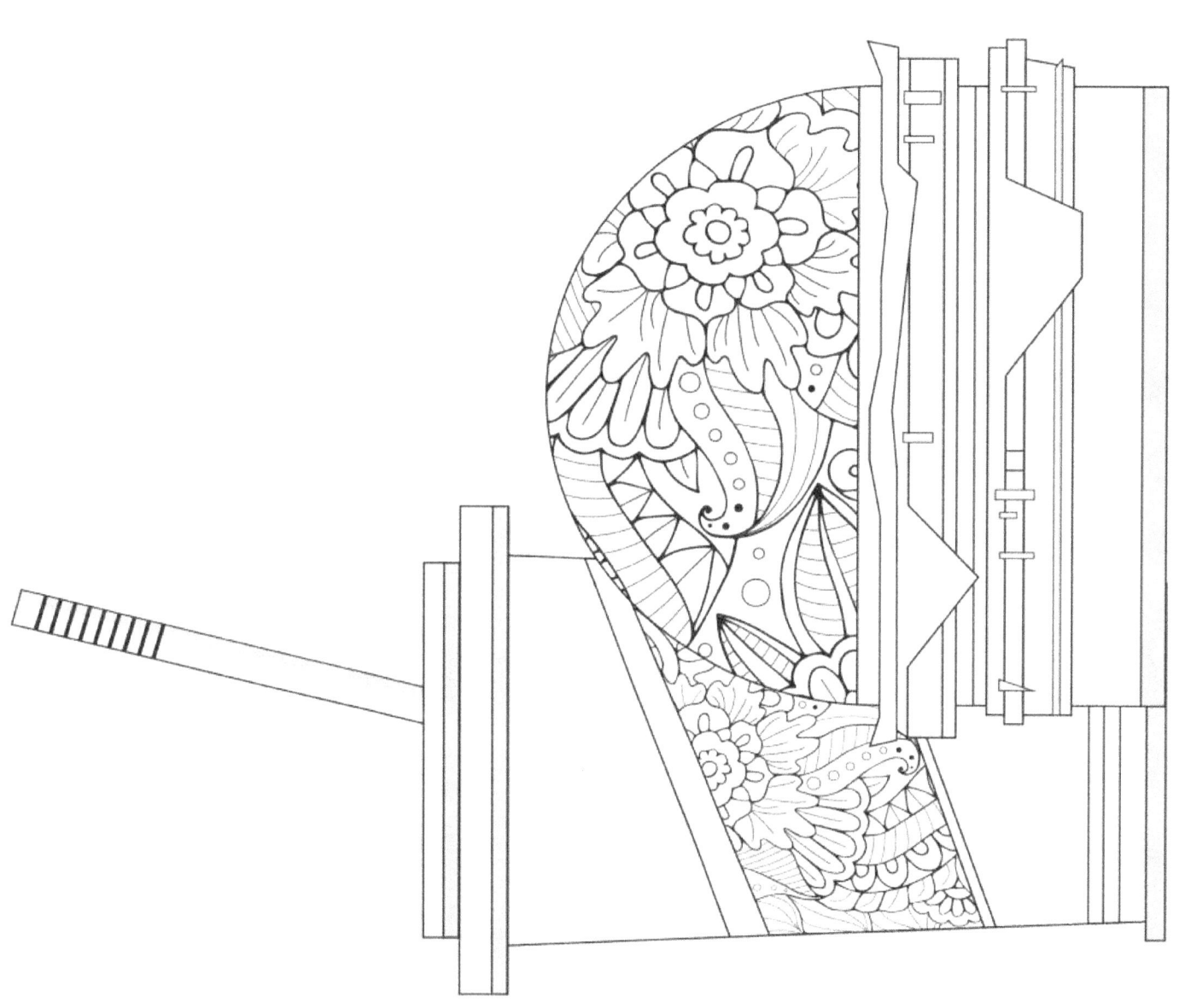

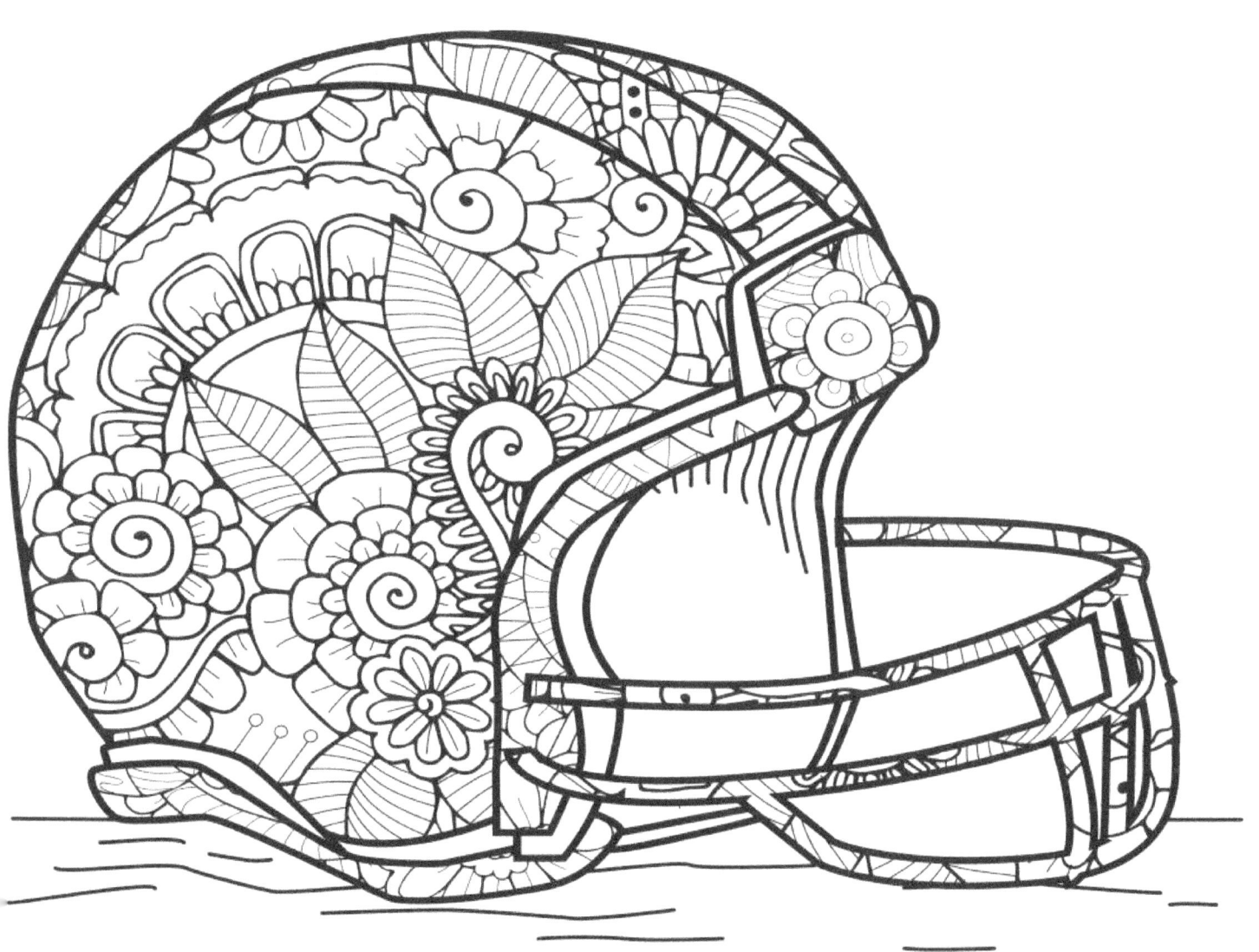

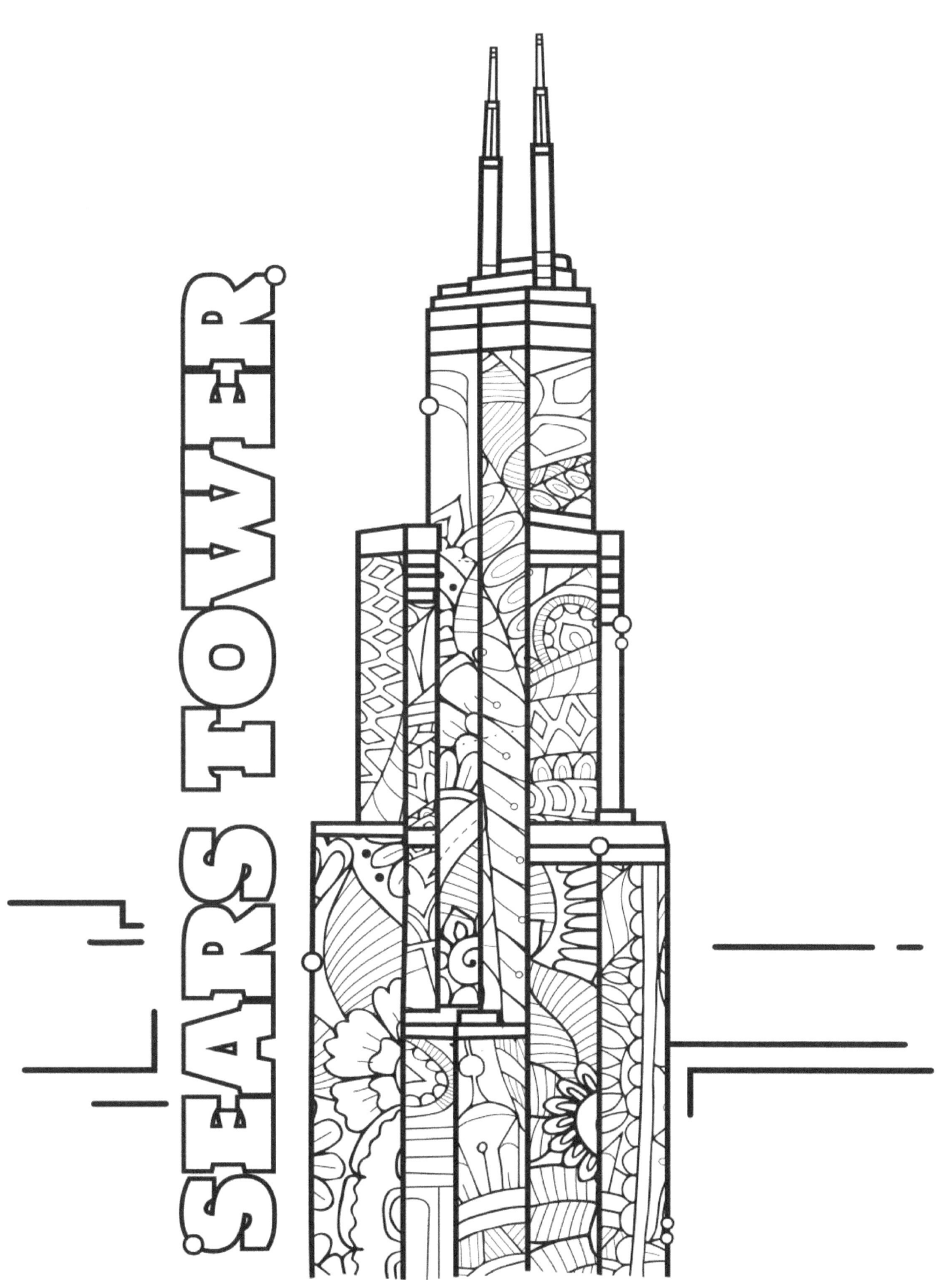

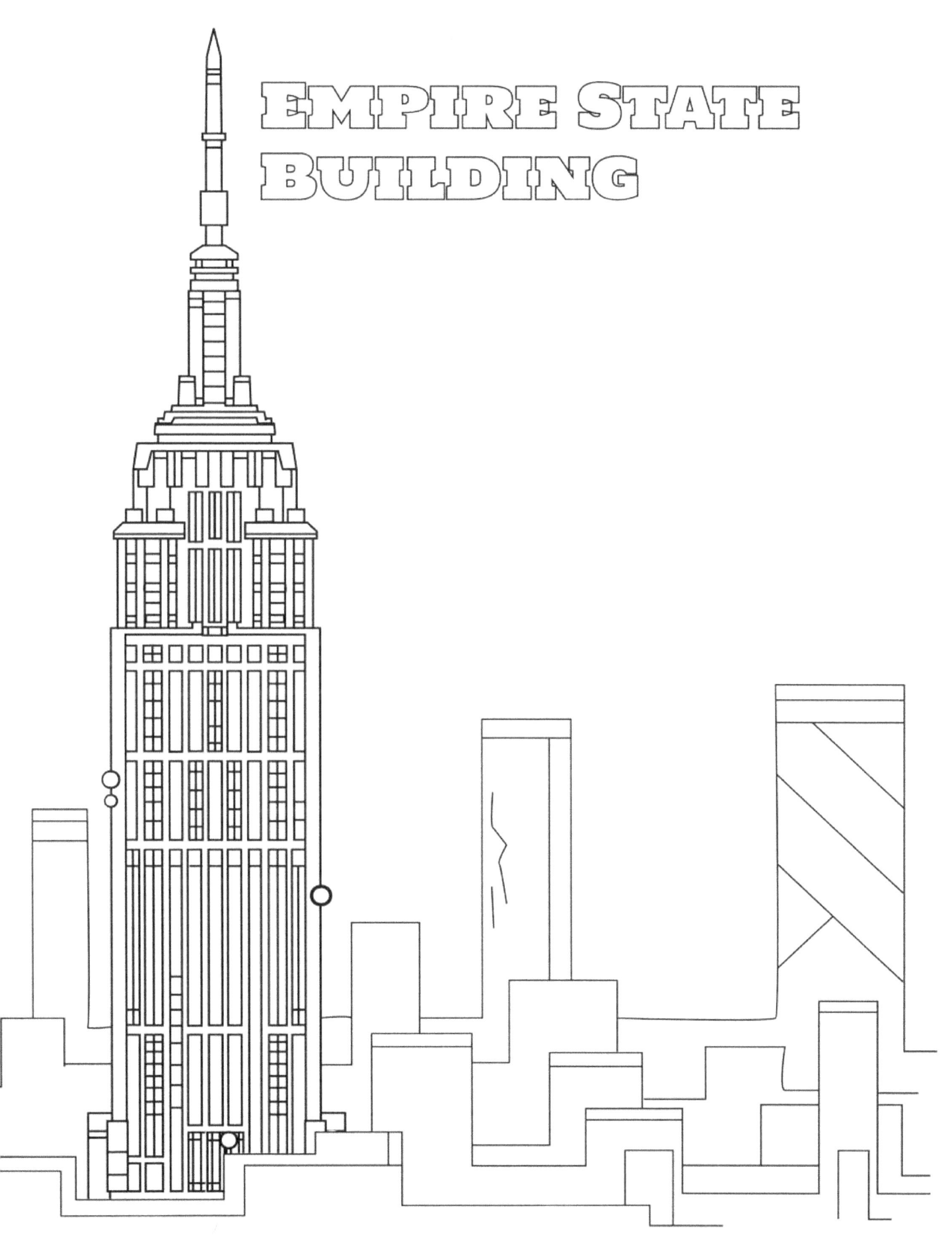

EMPIRE STATE BUILDING

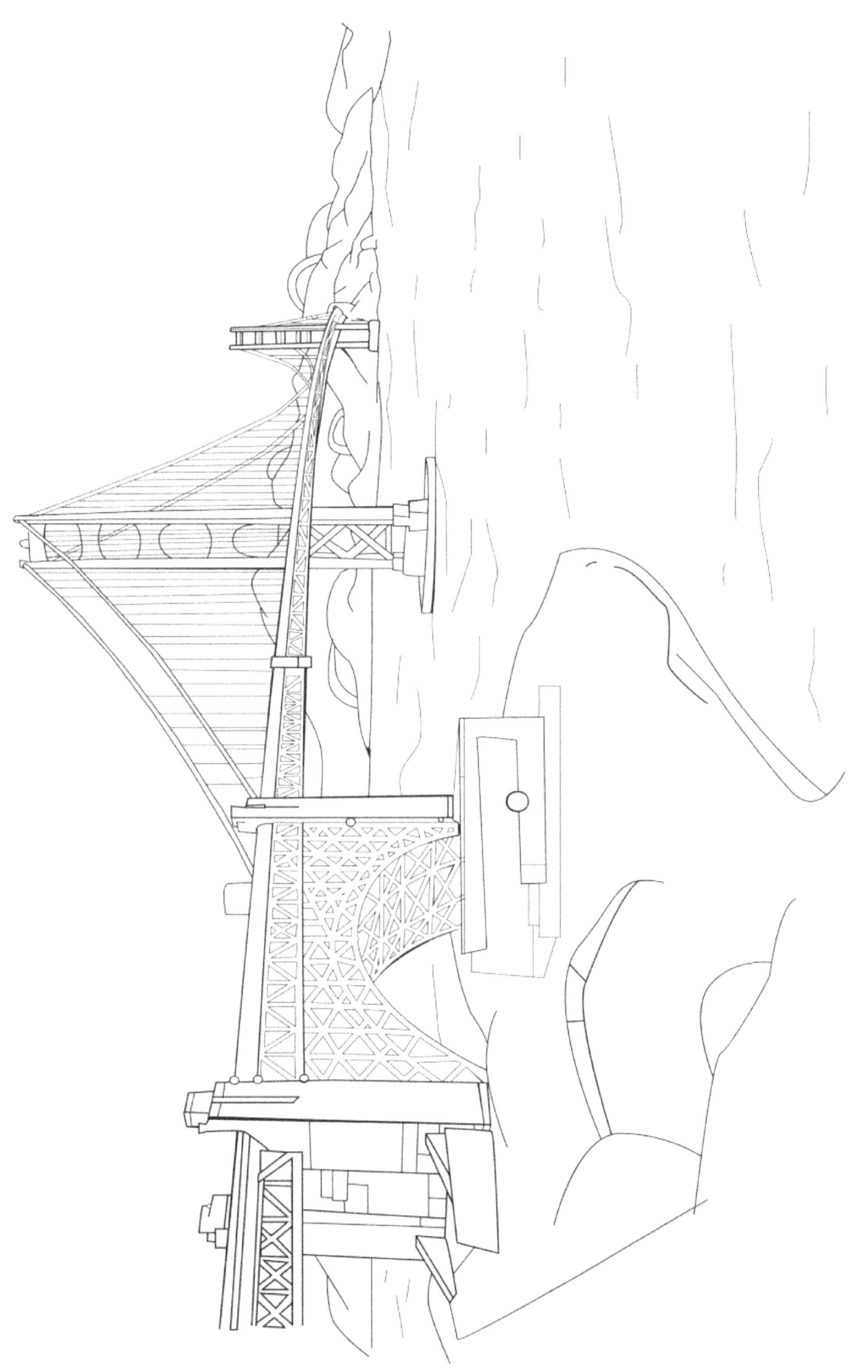

Happy Thanksgiving

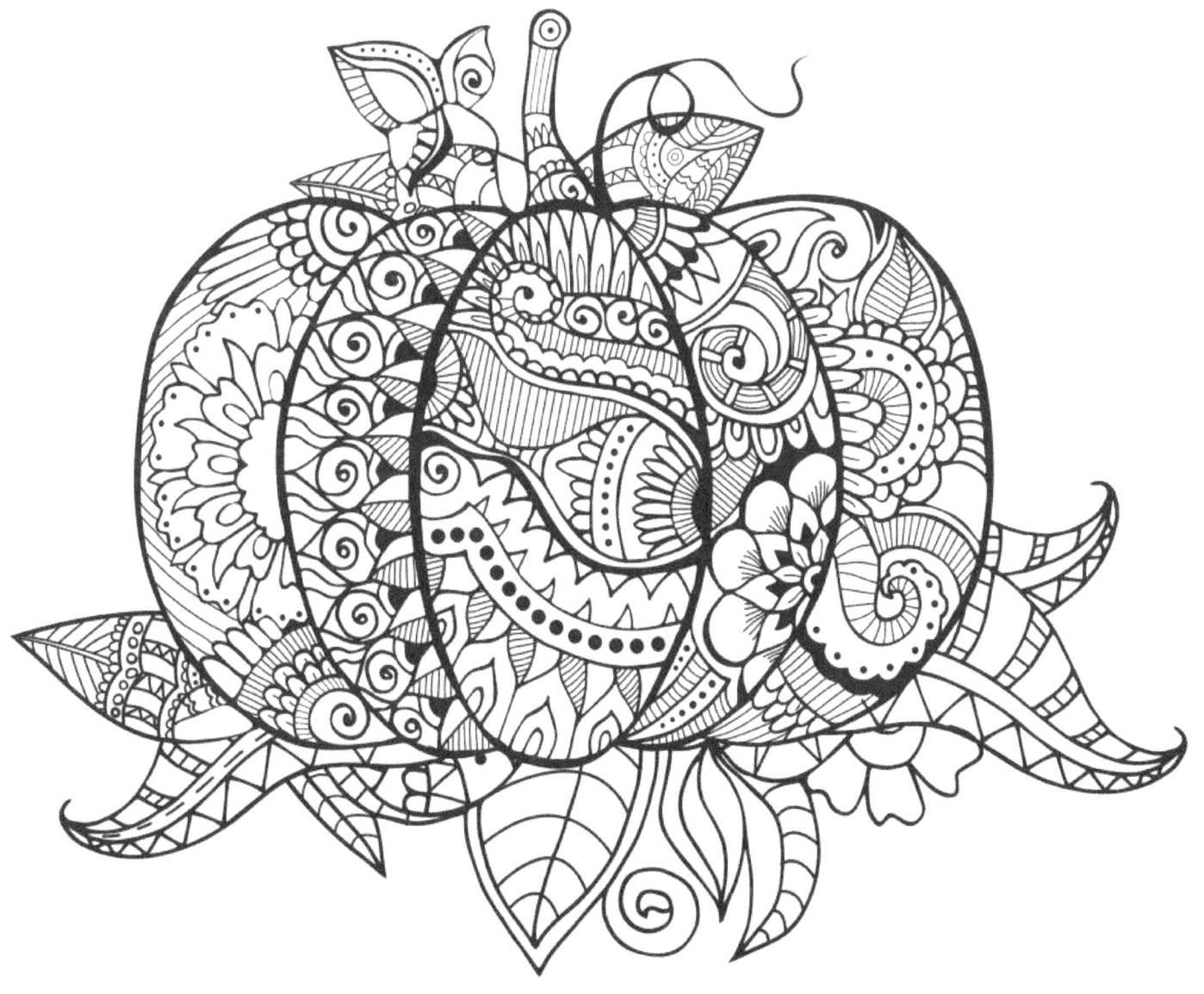

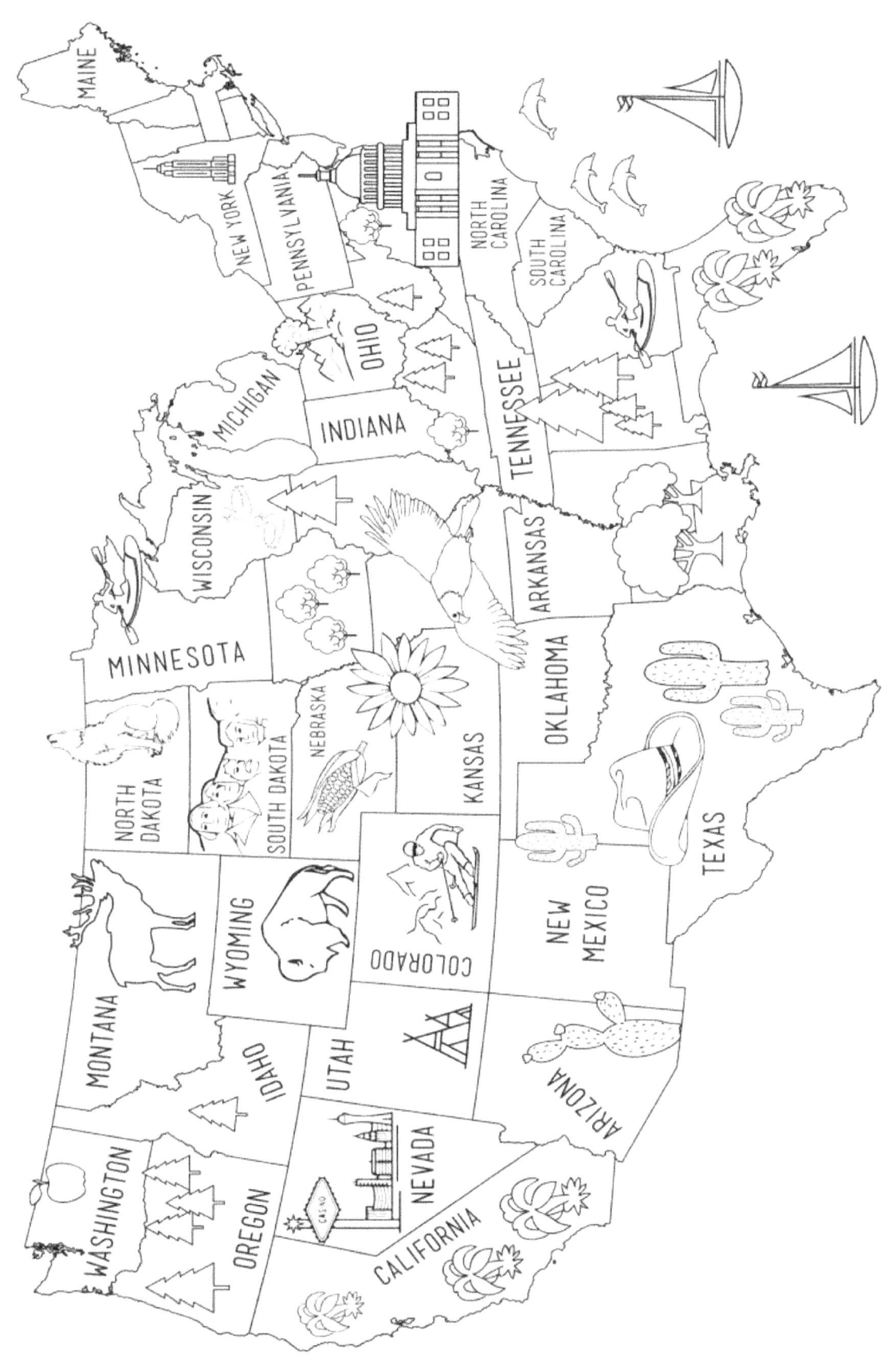

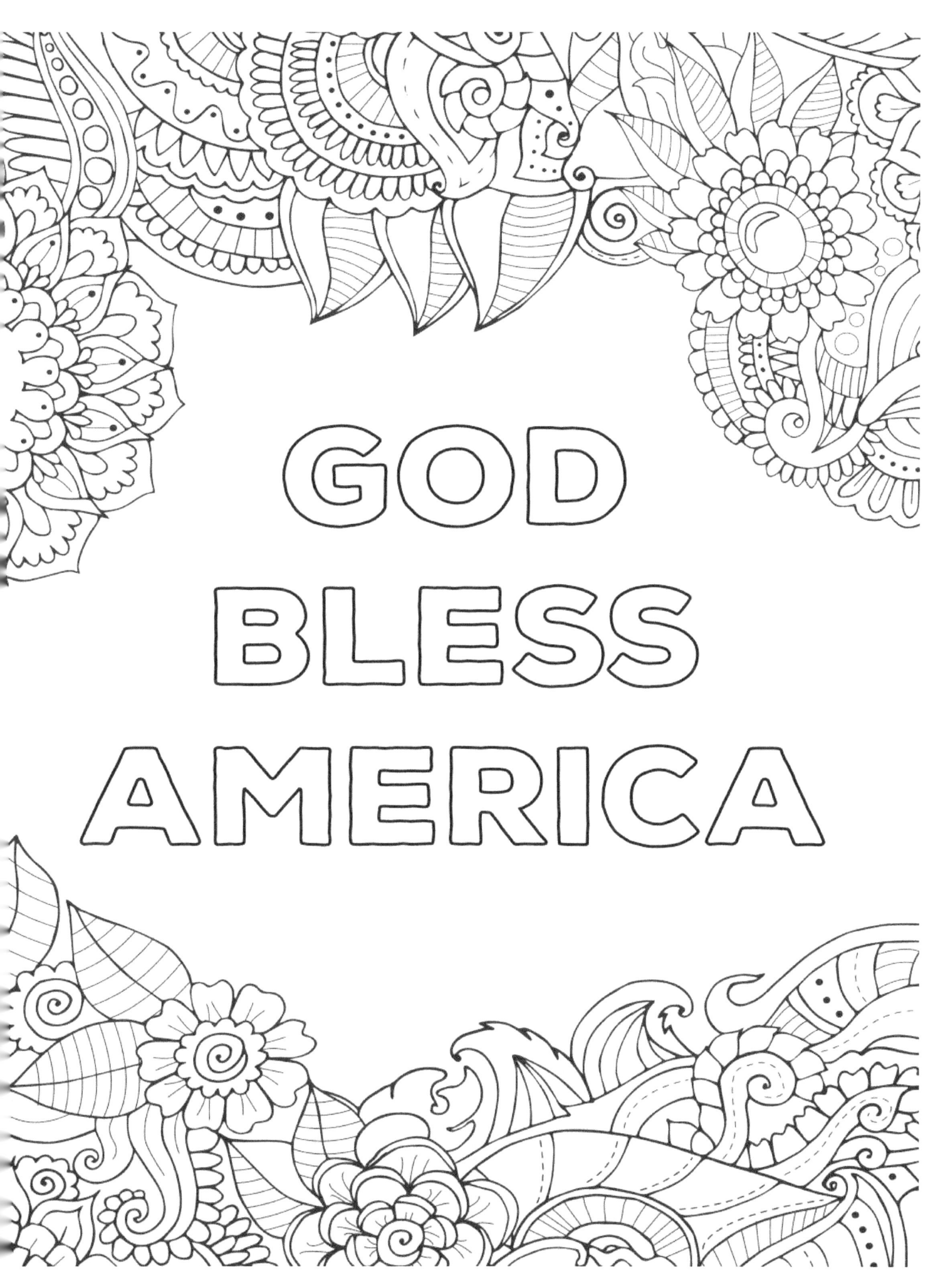

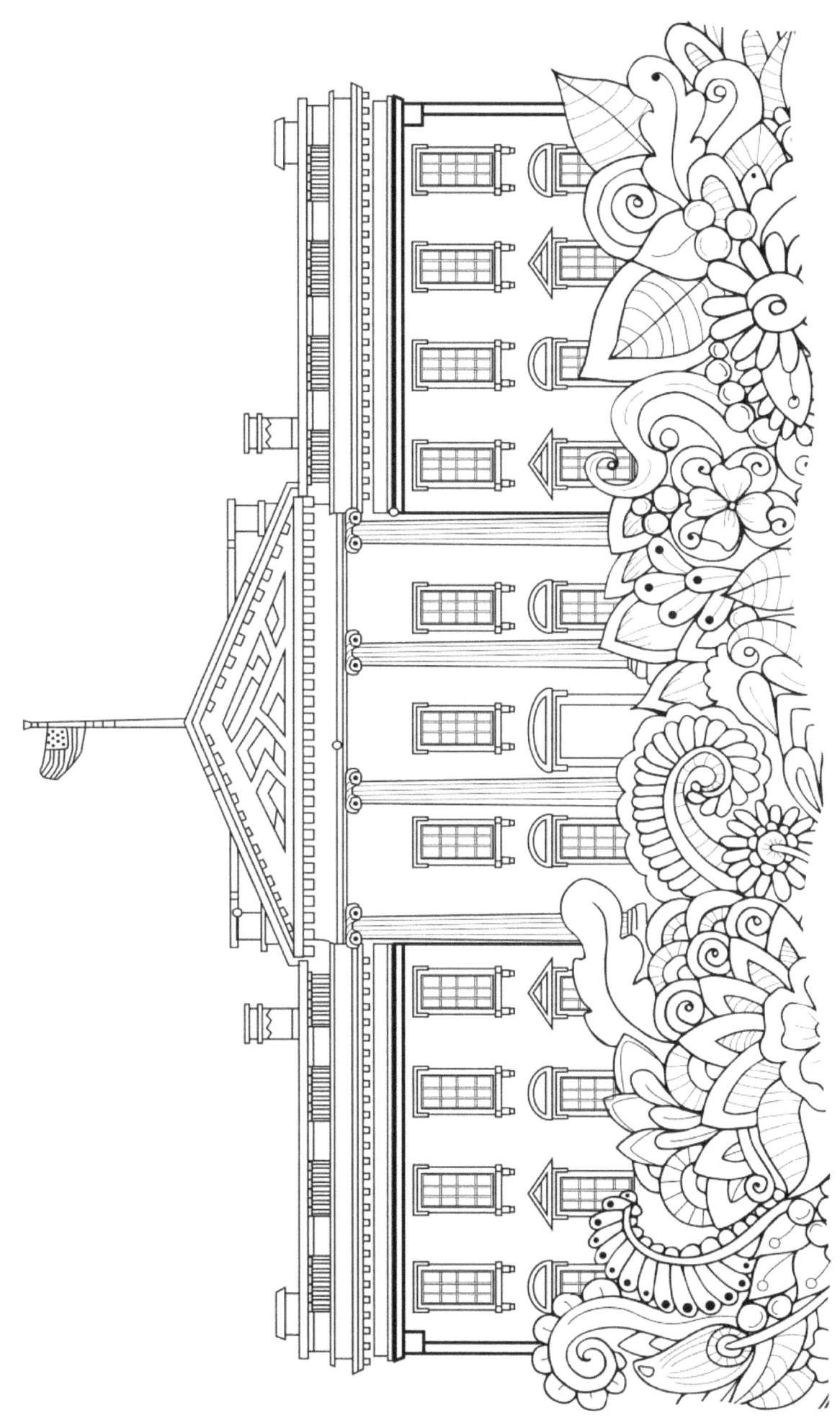

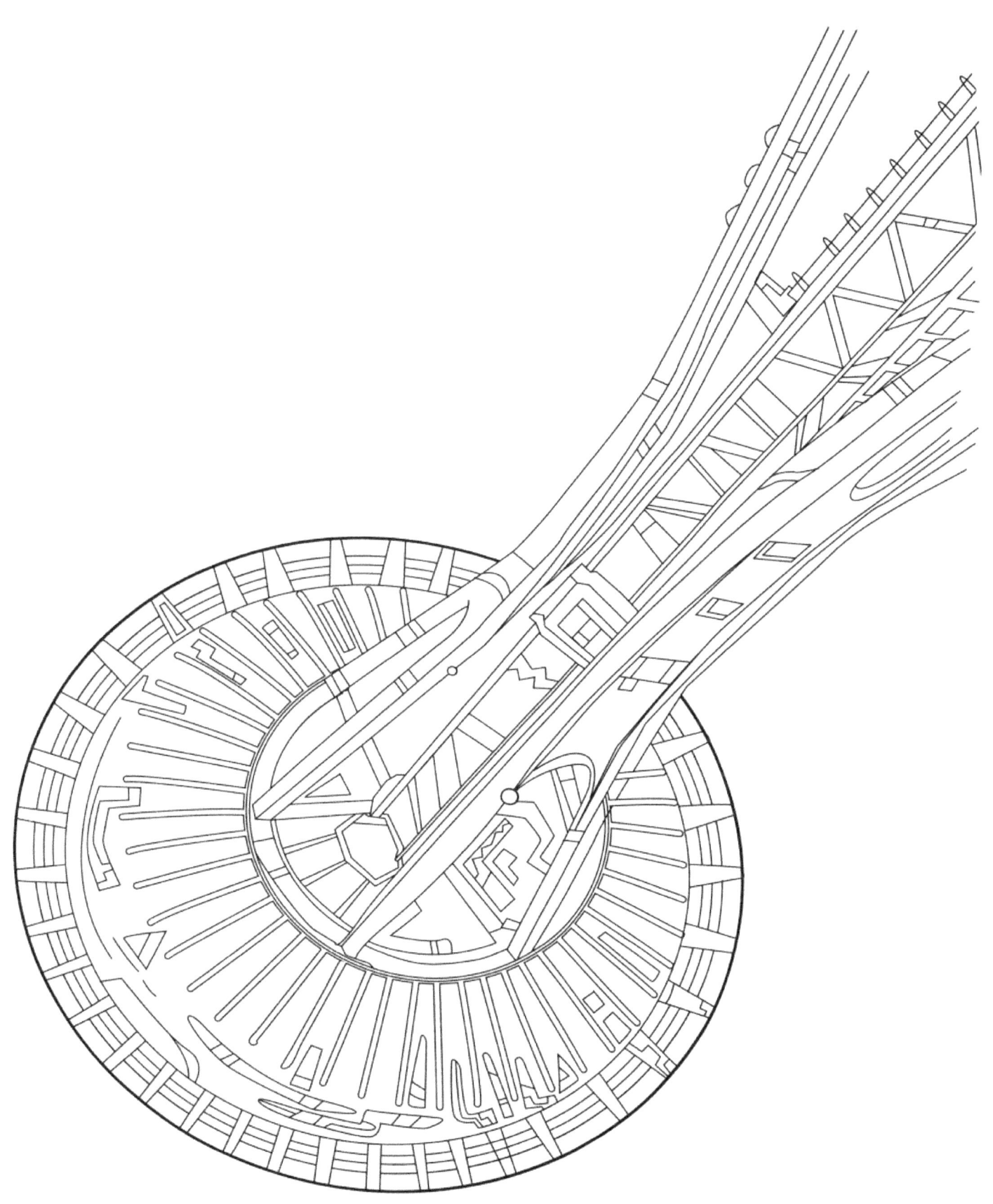

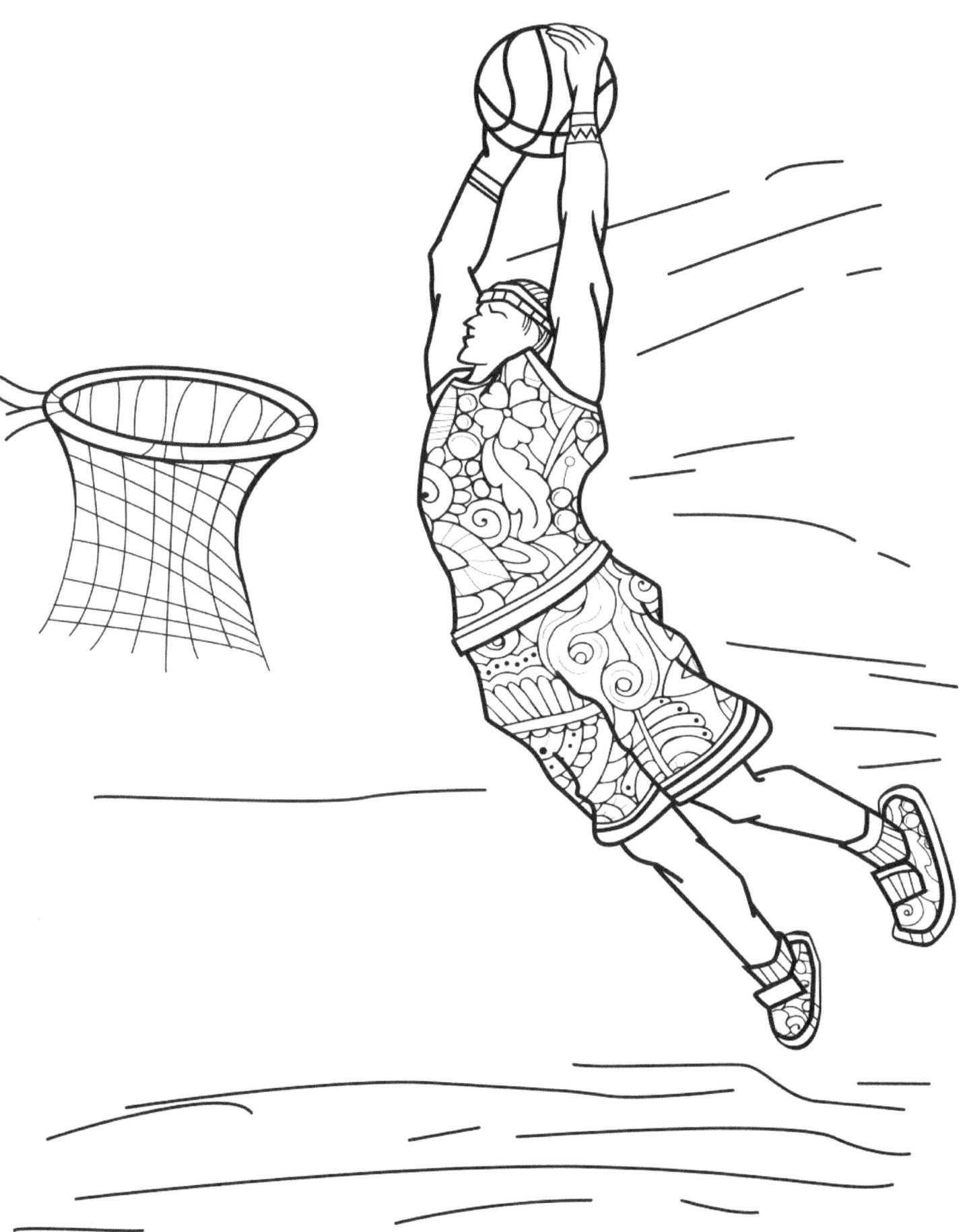

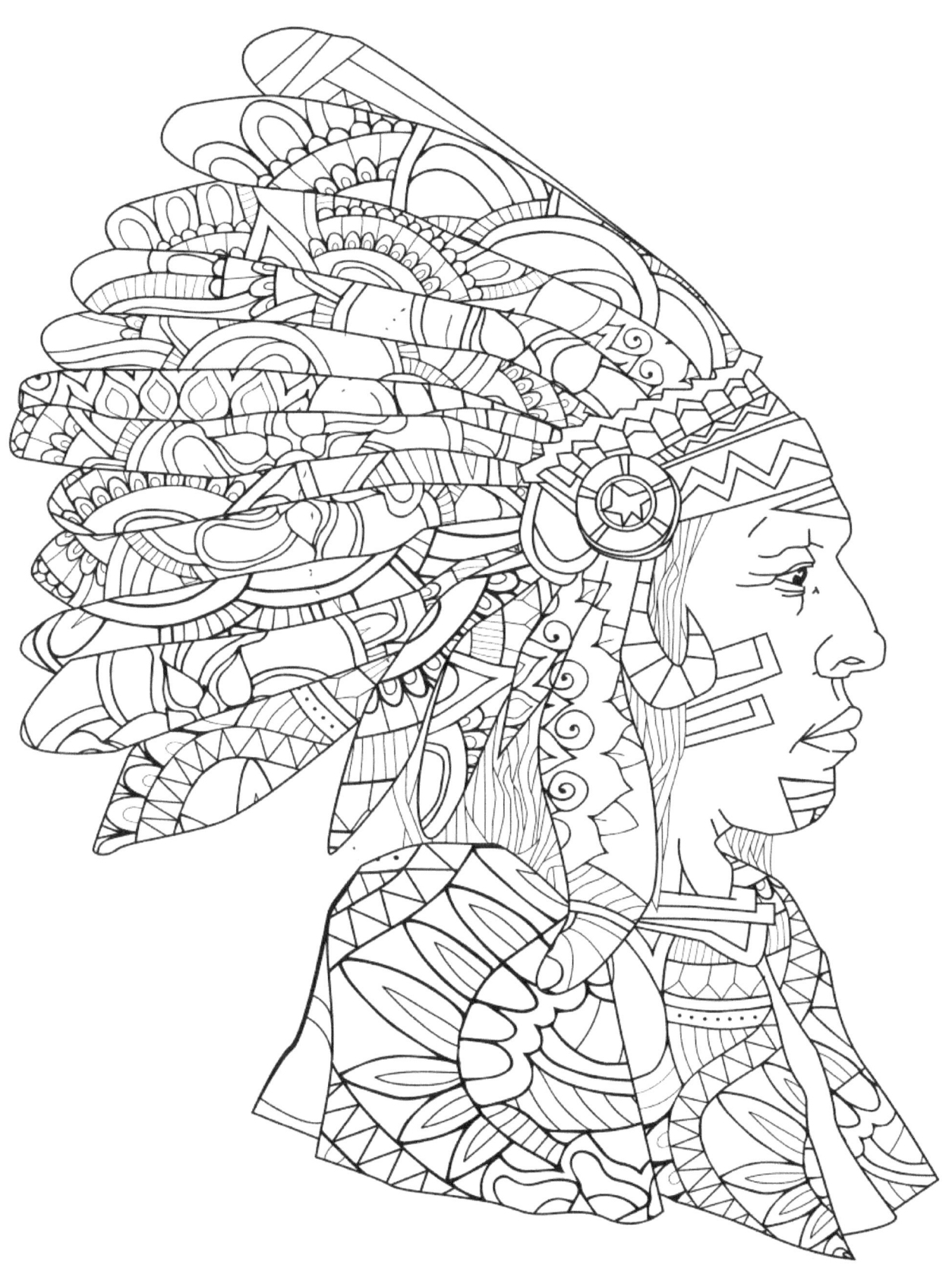

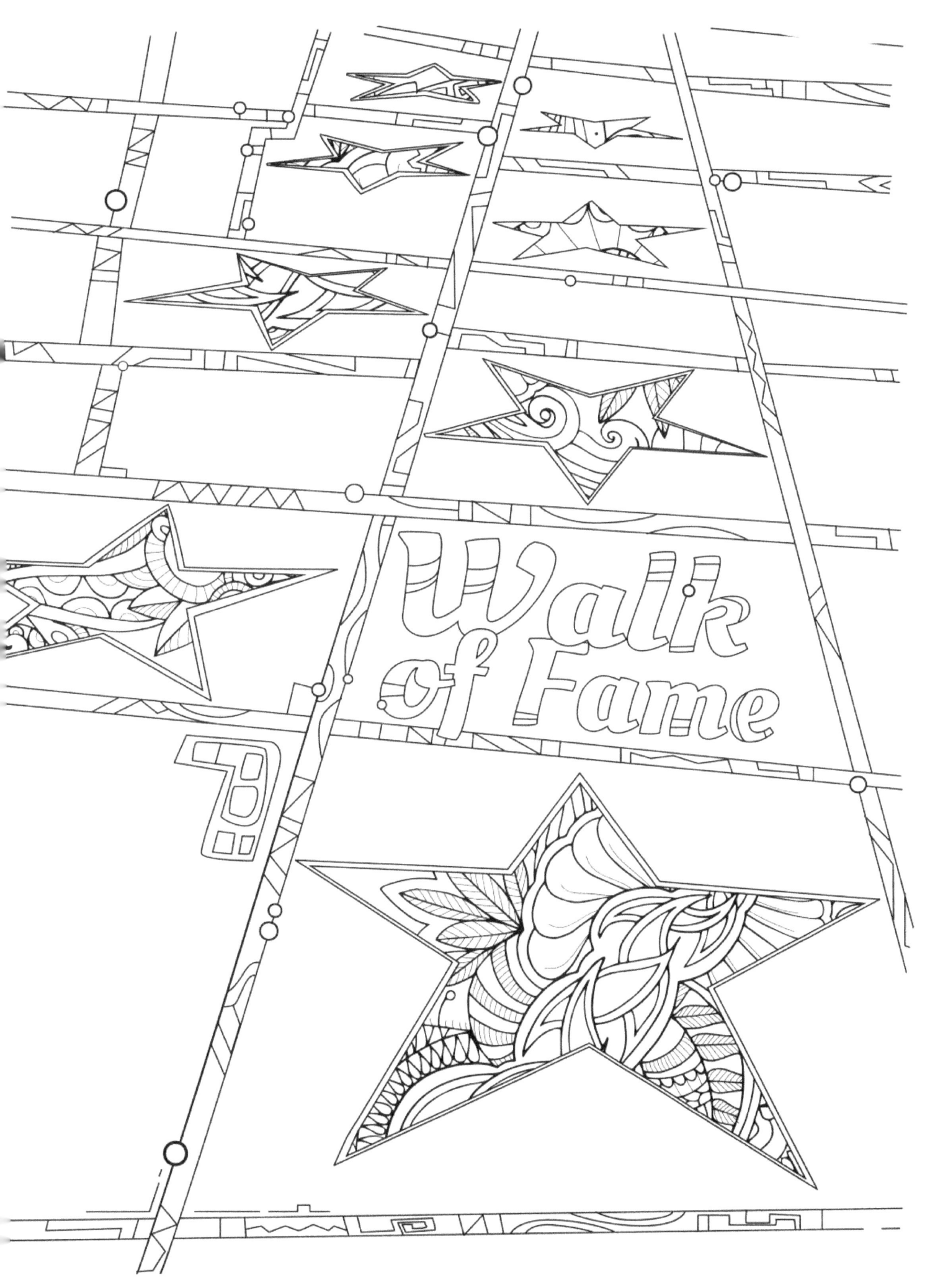

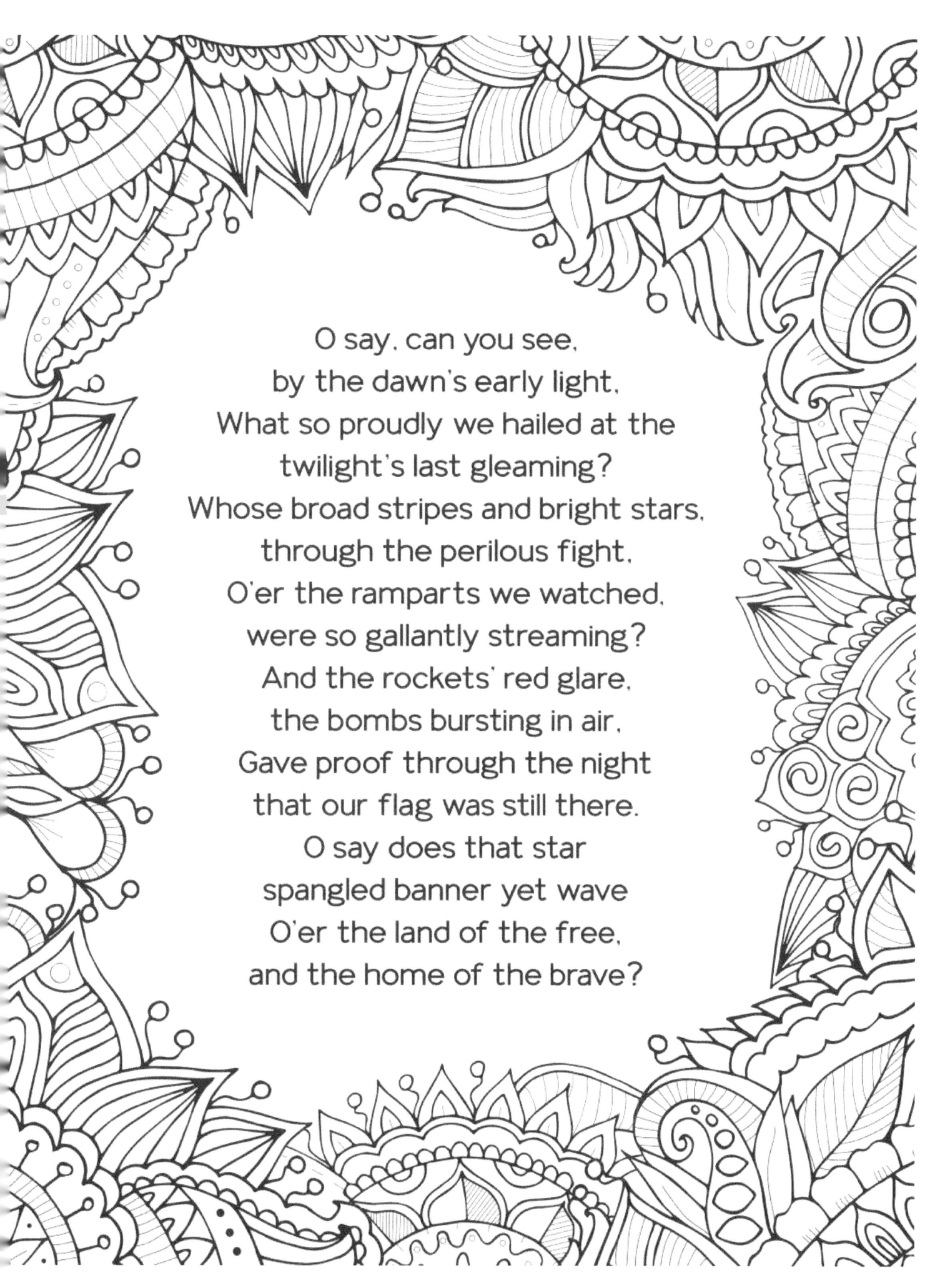

O say, can you see,
by the dawn's early light,
What so proudly we hailed at the
twilight's last gleaming?
Whose broad stripes and bright stars,
through the perilous fight,
O'er the ramparts we watched,
were so gallantly streaming?
And the rockets' red glare,
the bombs bursting in air,
Gave proof through the night
that our flag was still there.
O say does that star
spangled banner yet wave
O'er the land of the free,
and the home of the brave?

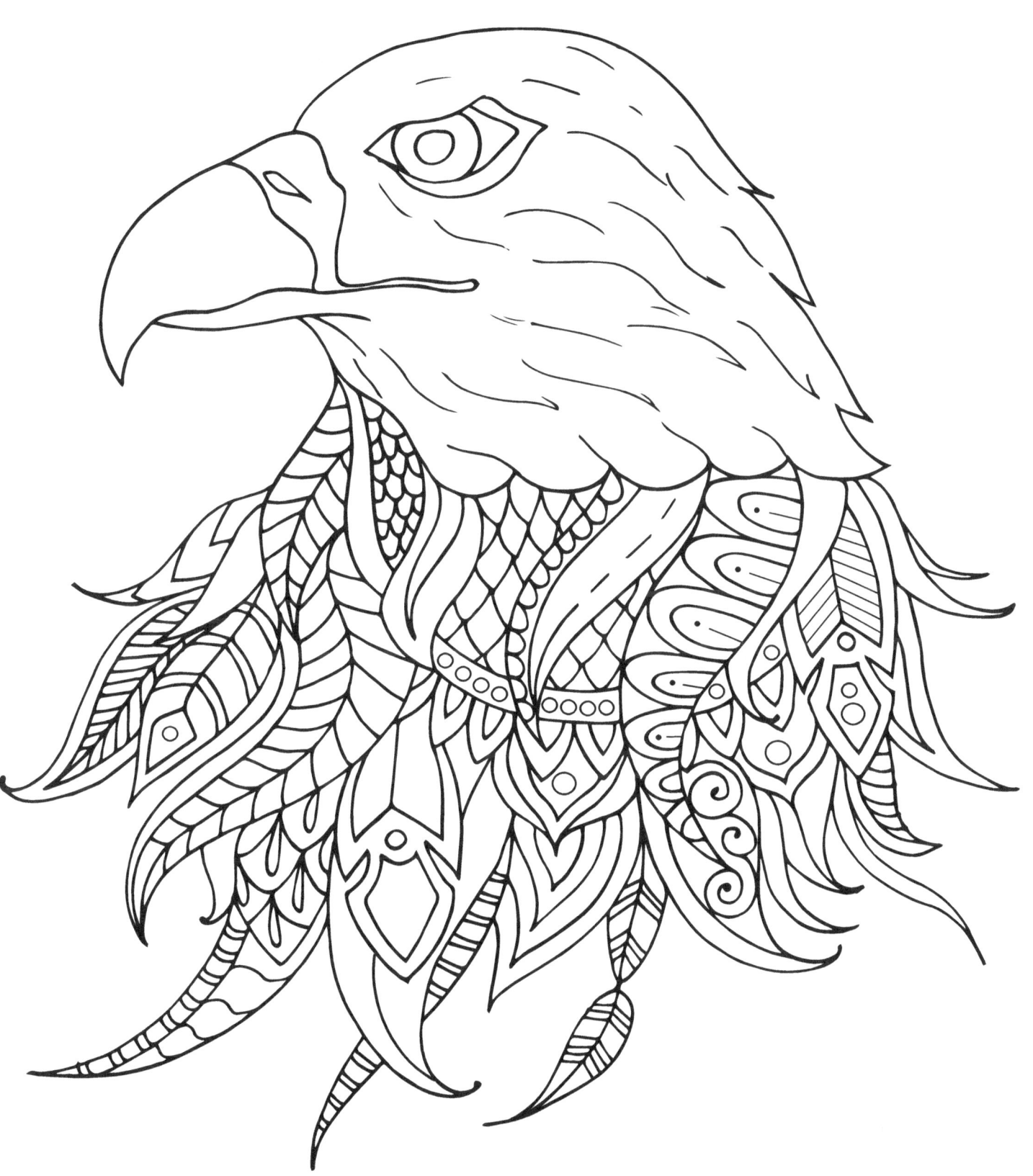

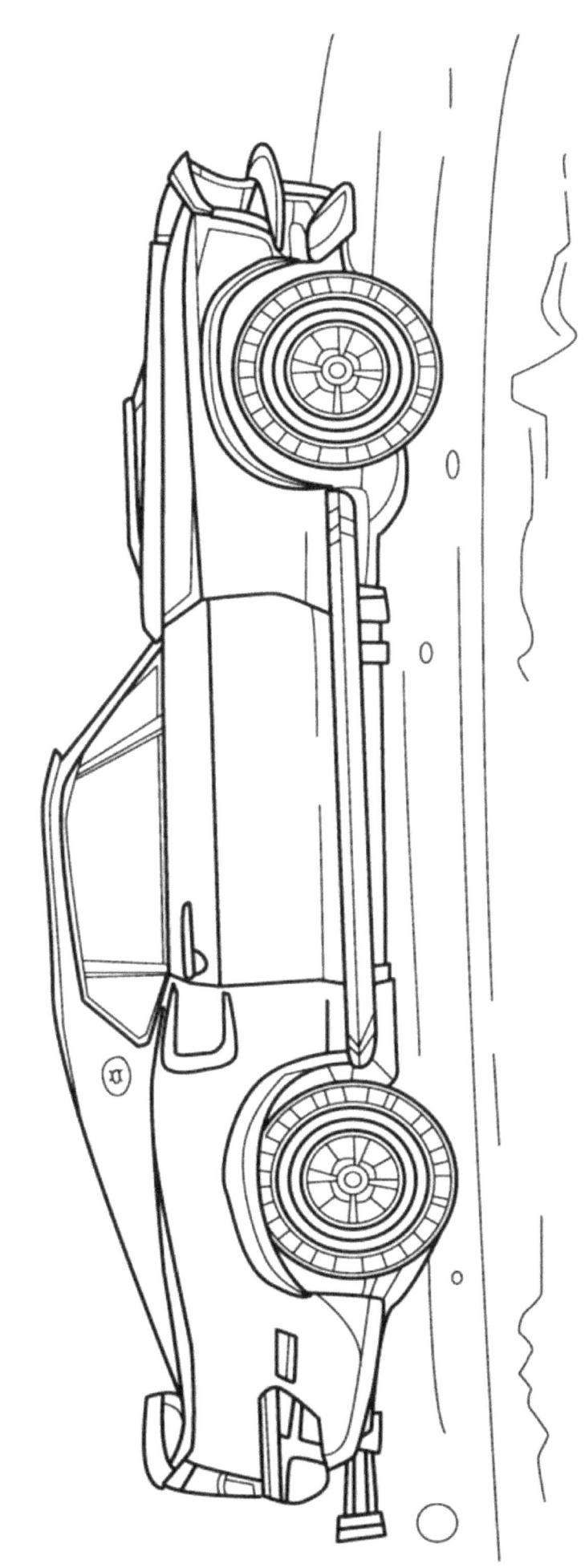

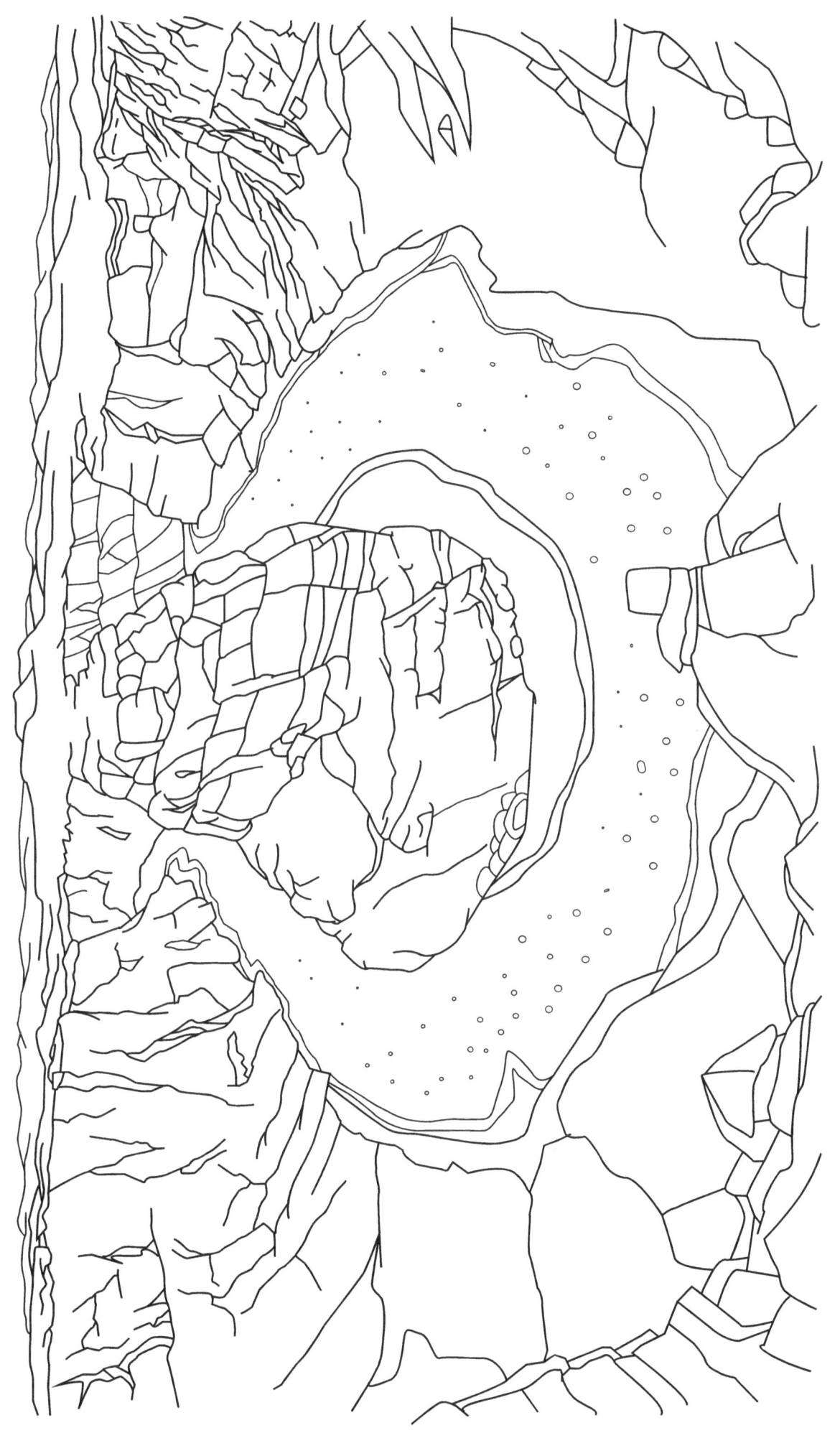

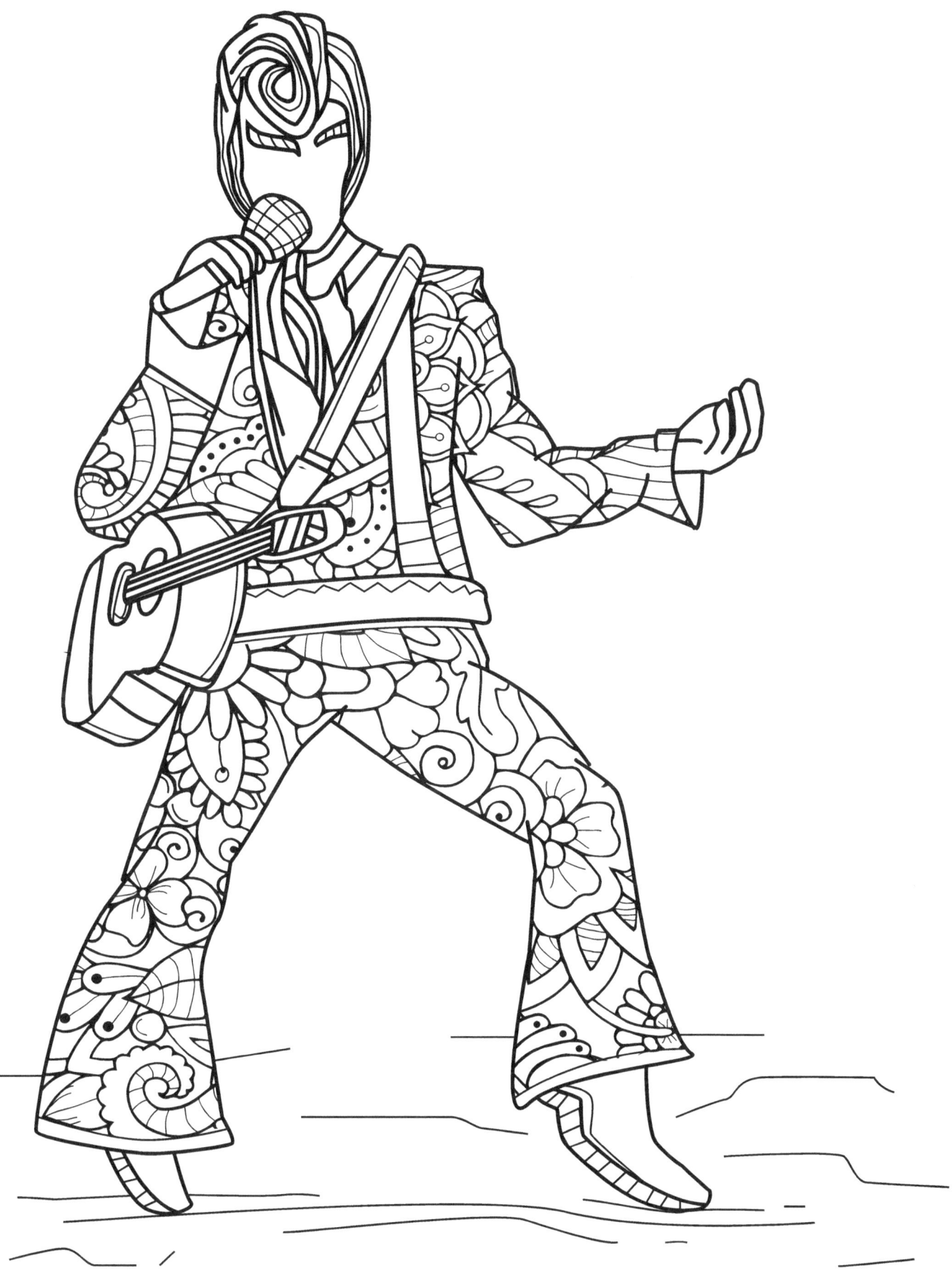

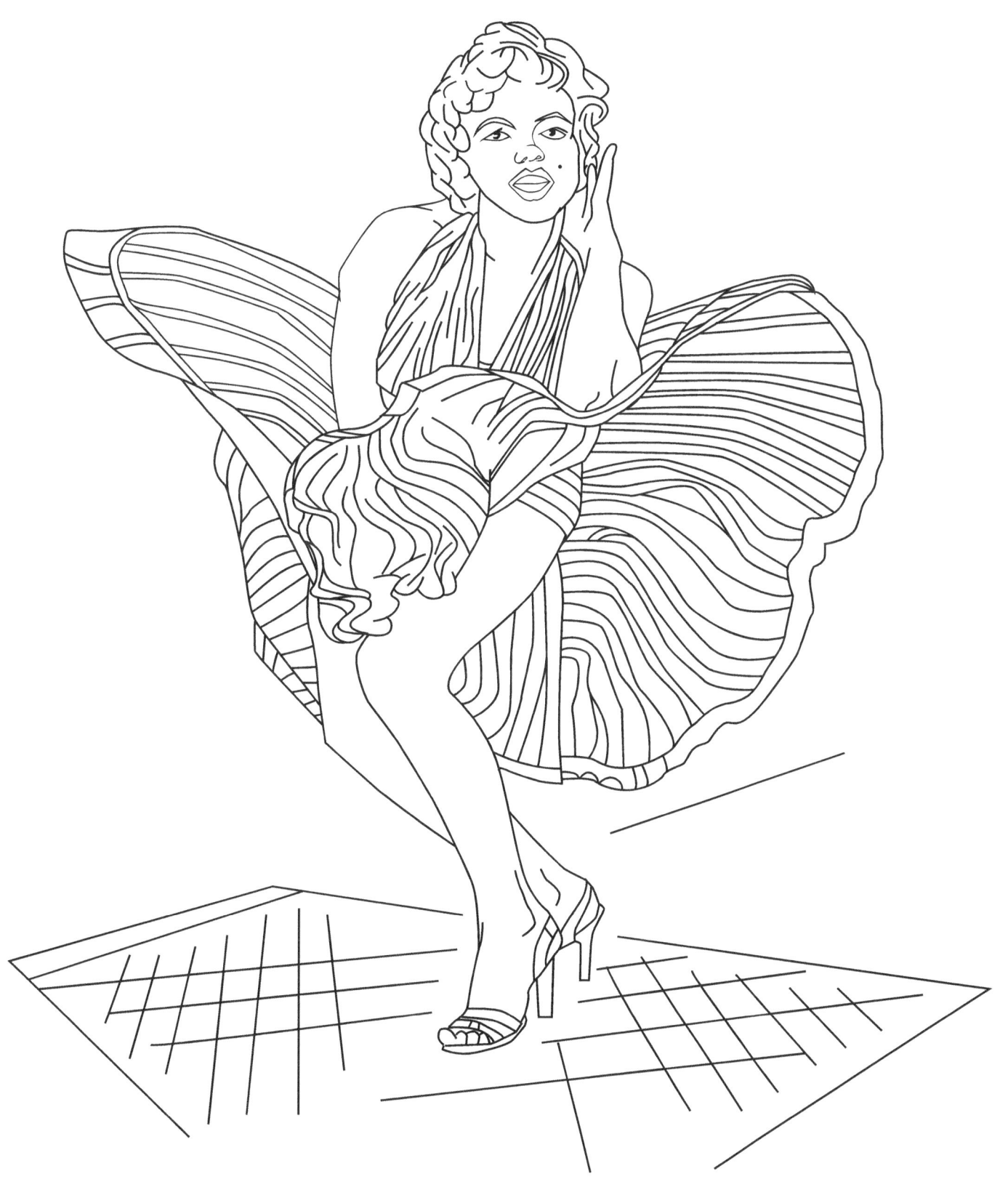

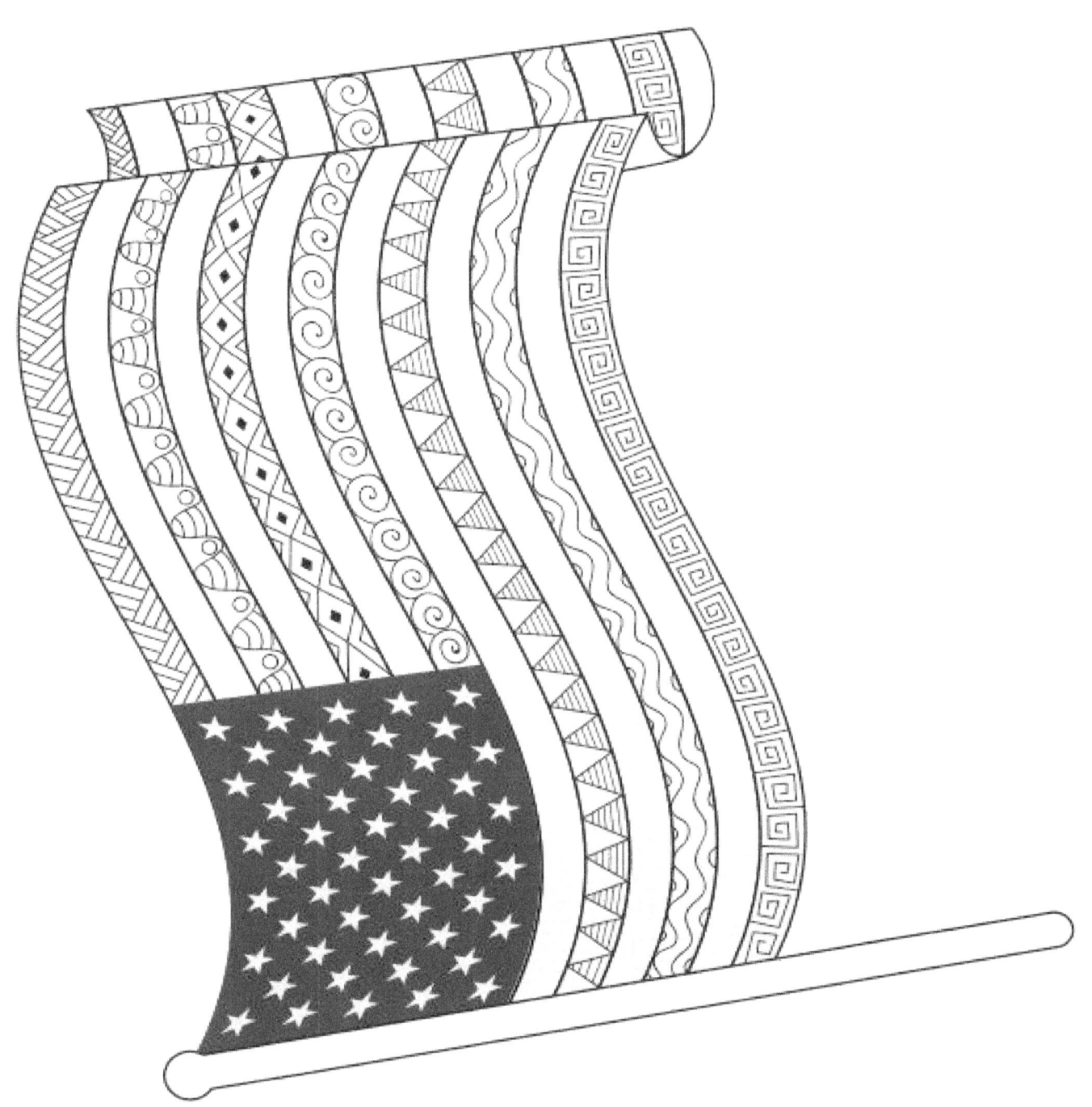

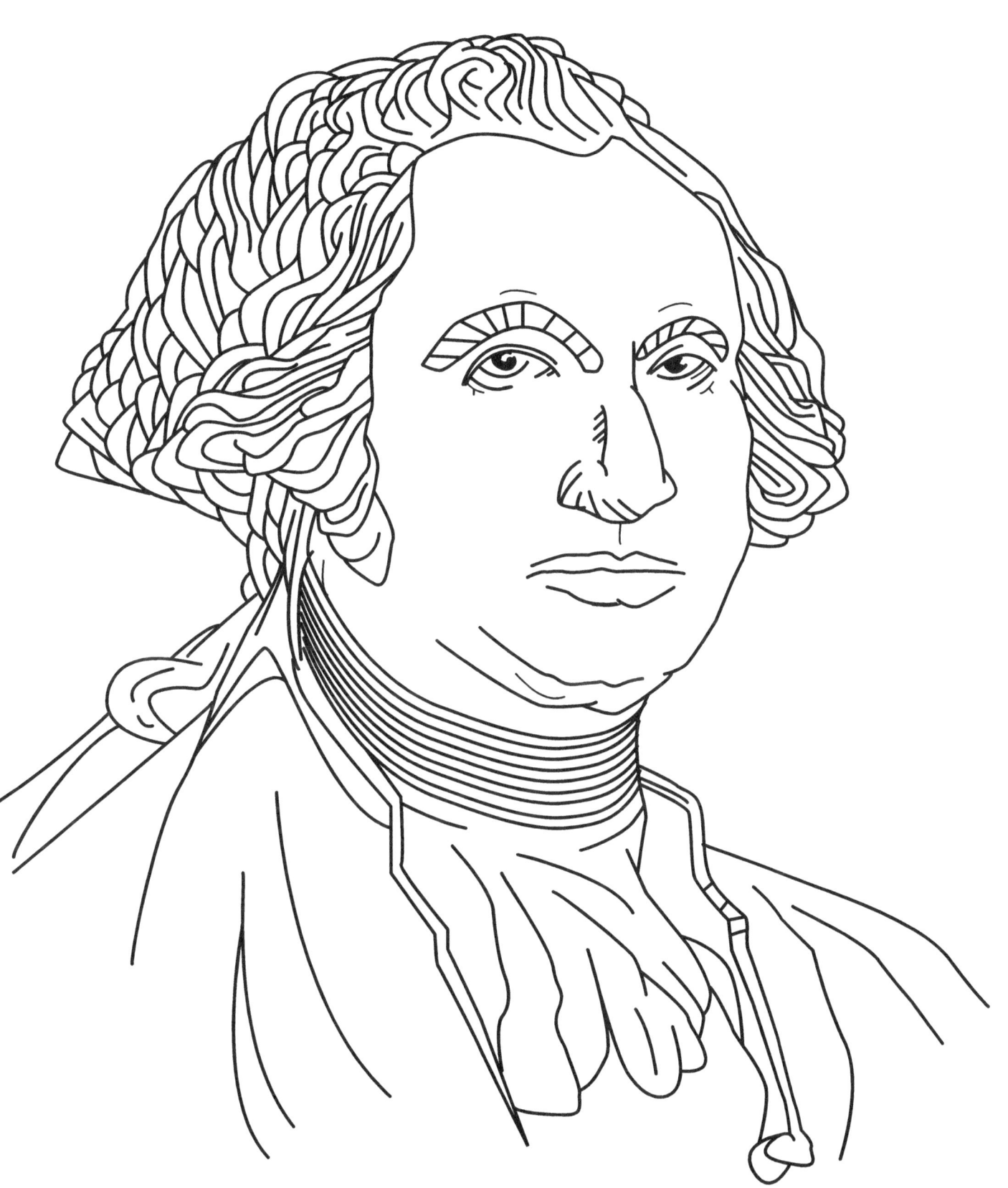

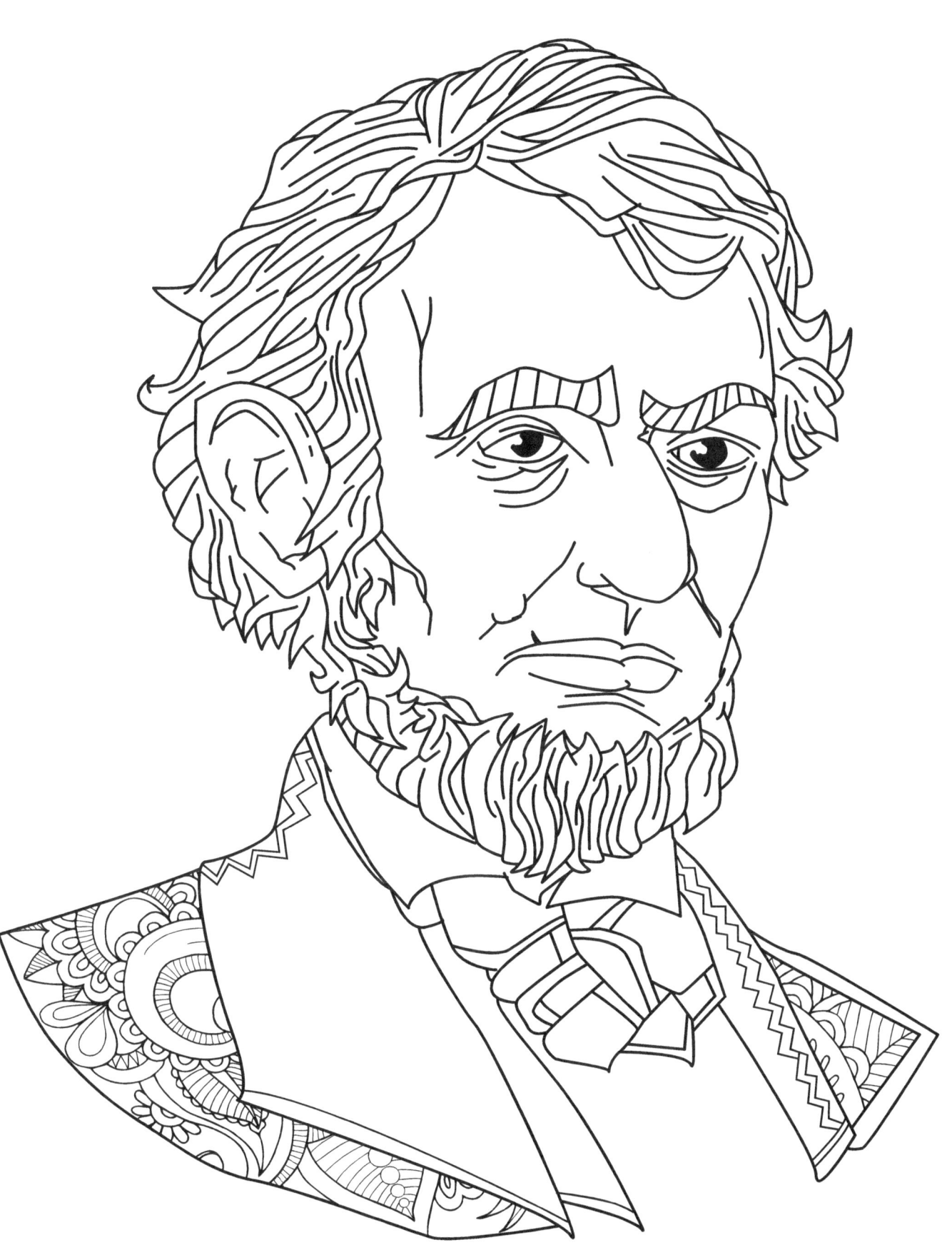

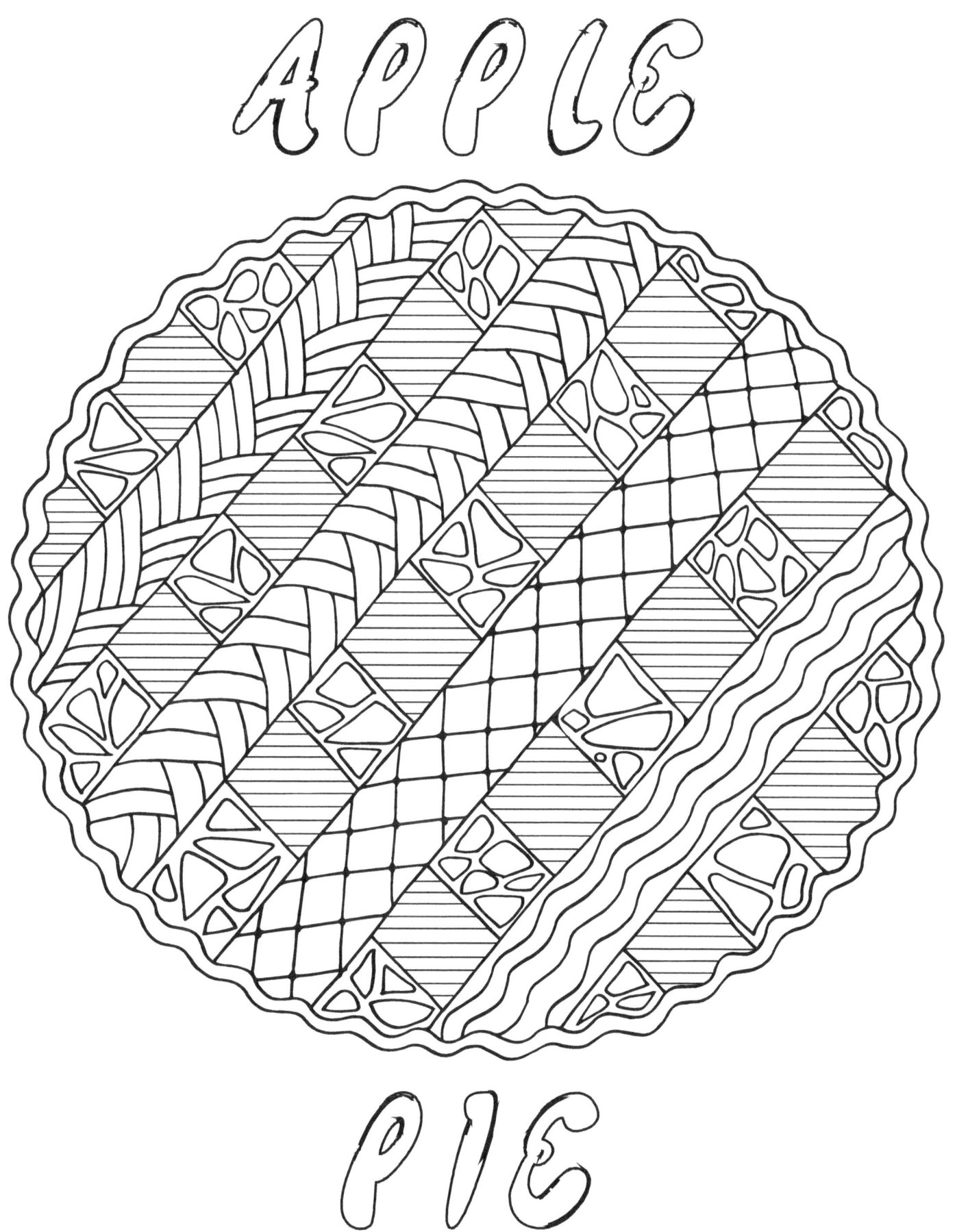

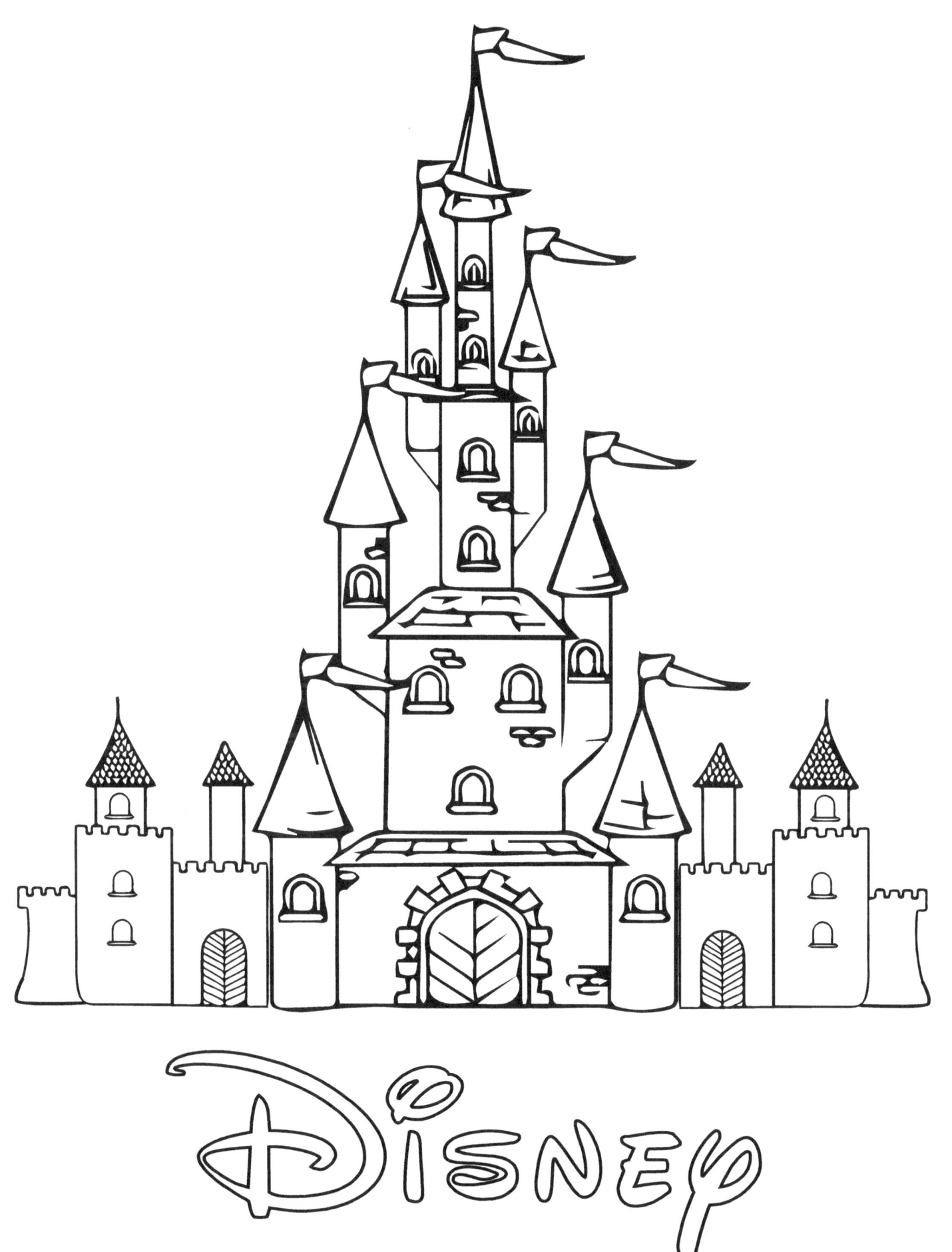

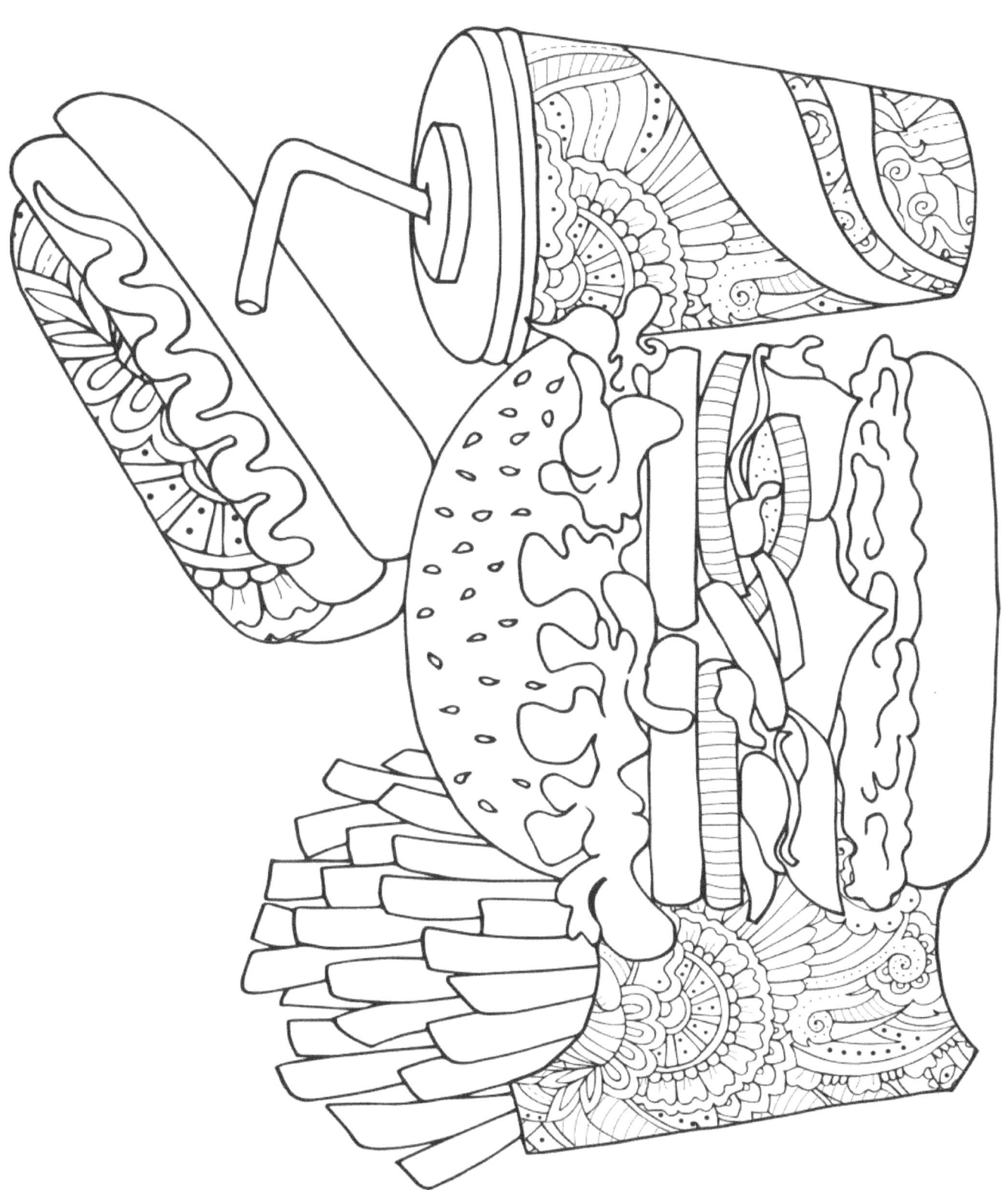

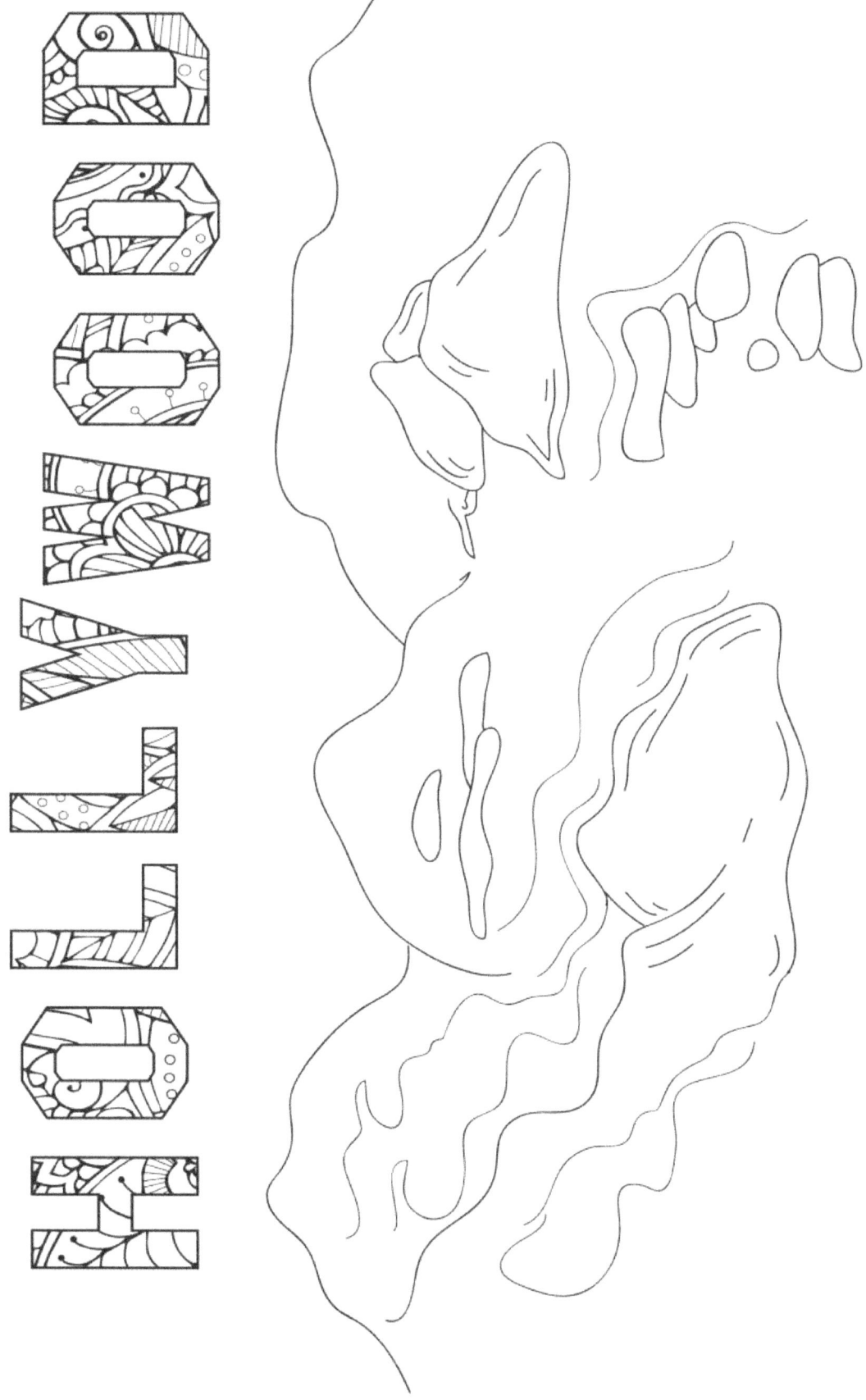

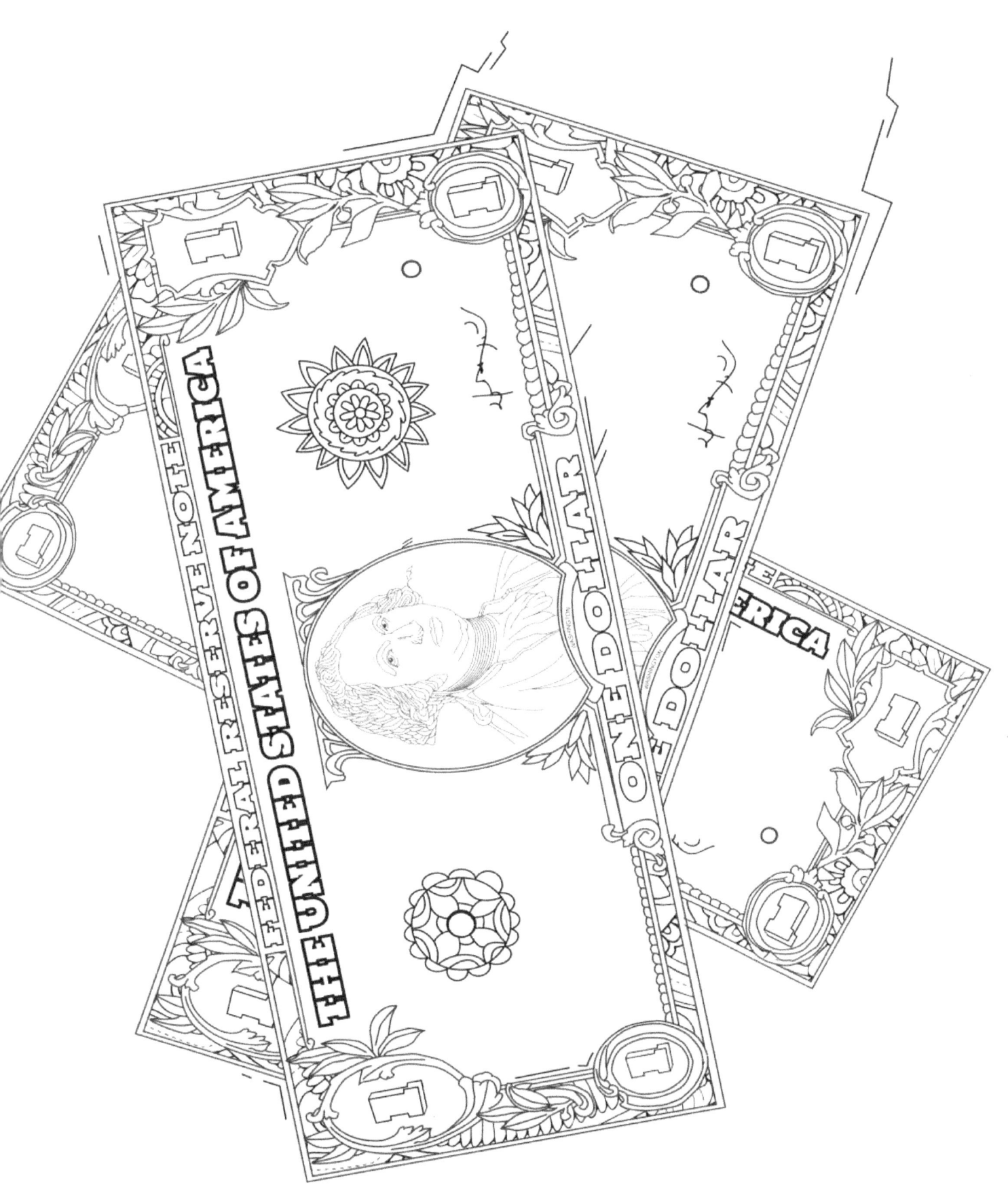

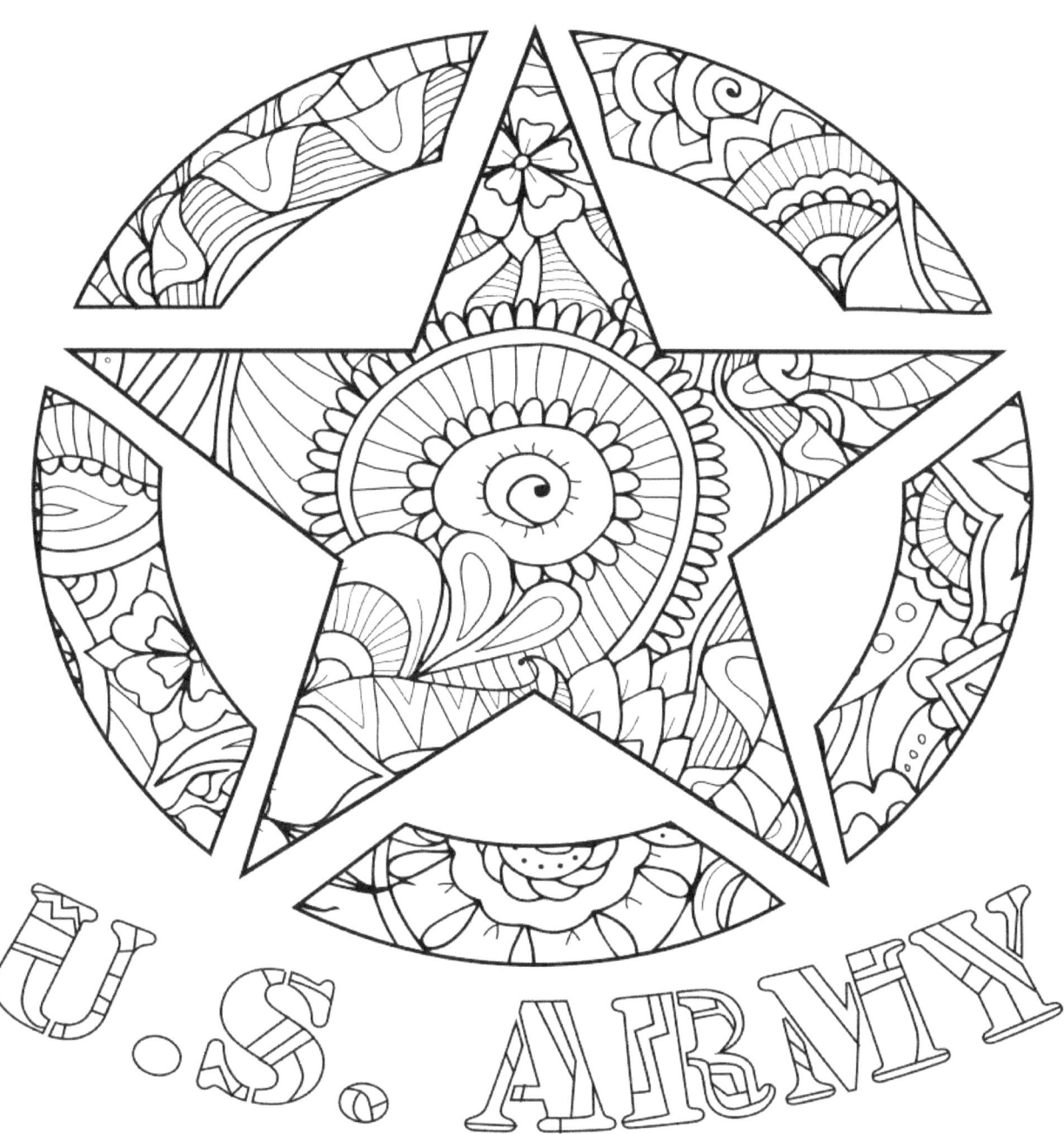

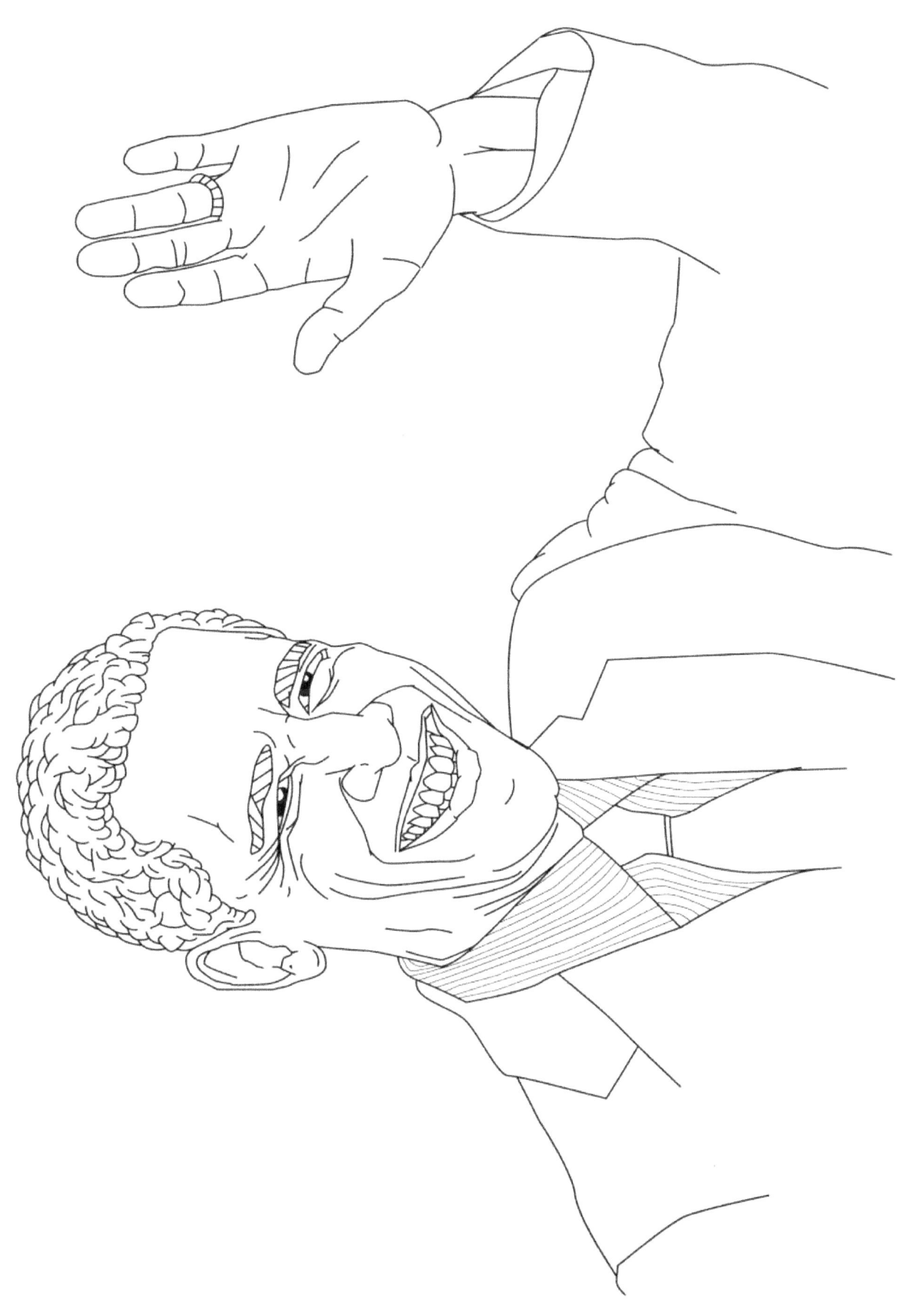

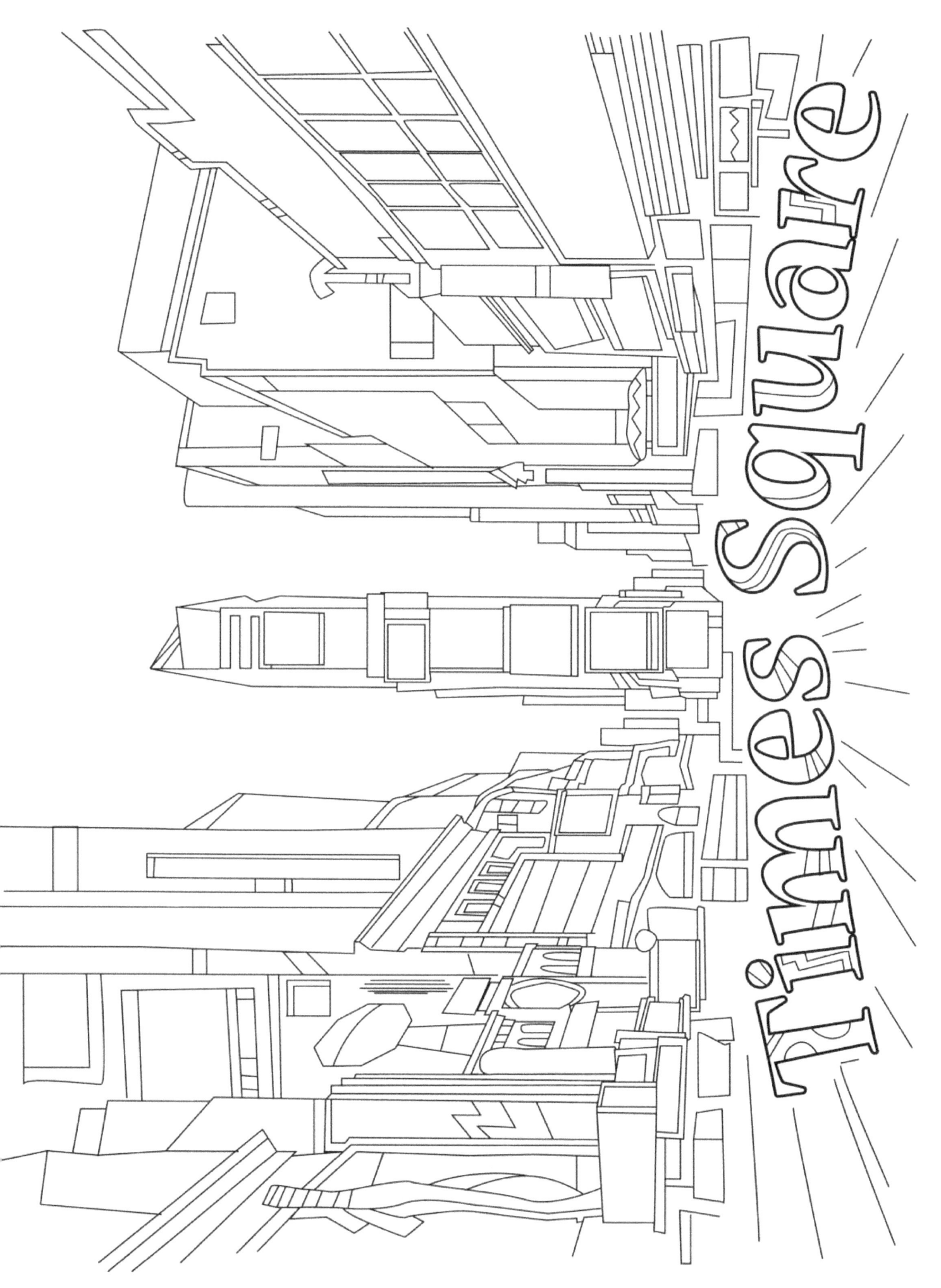

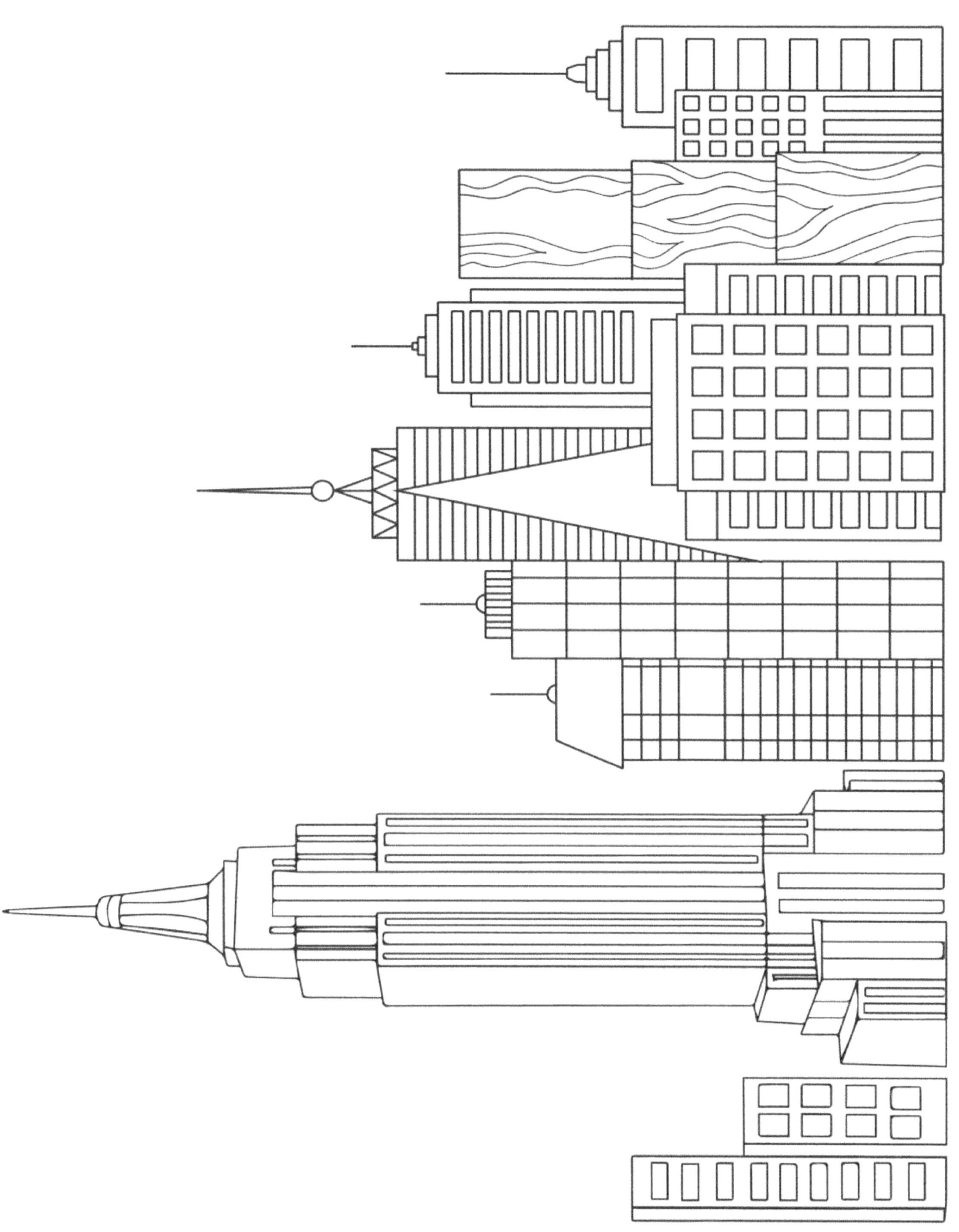

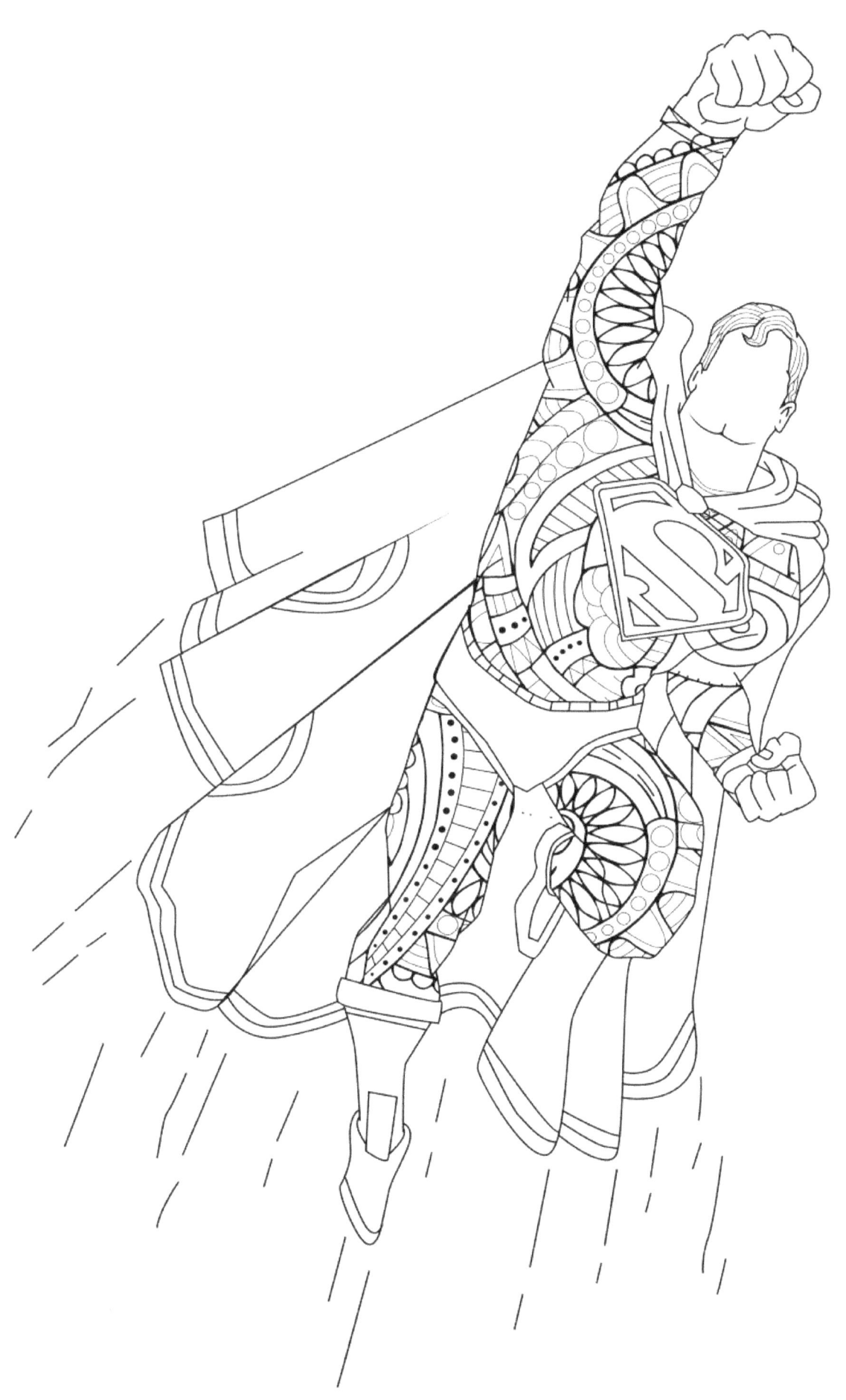

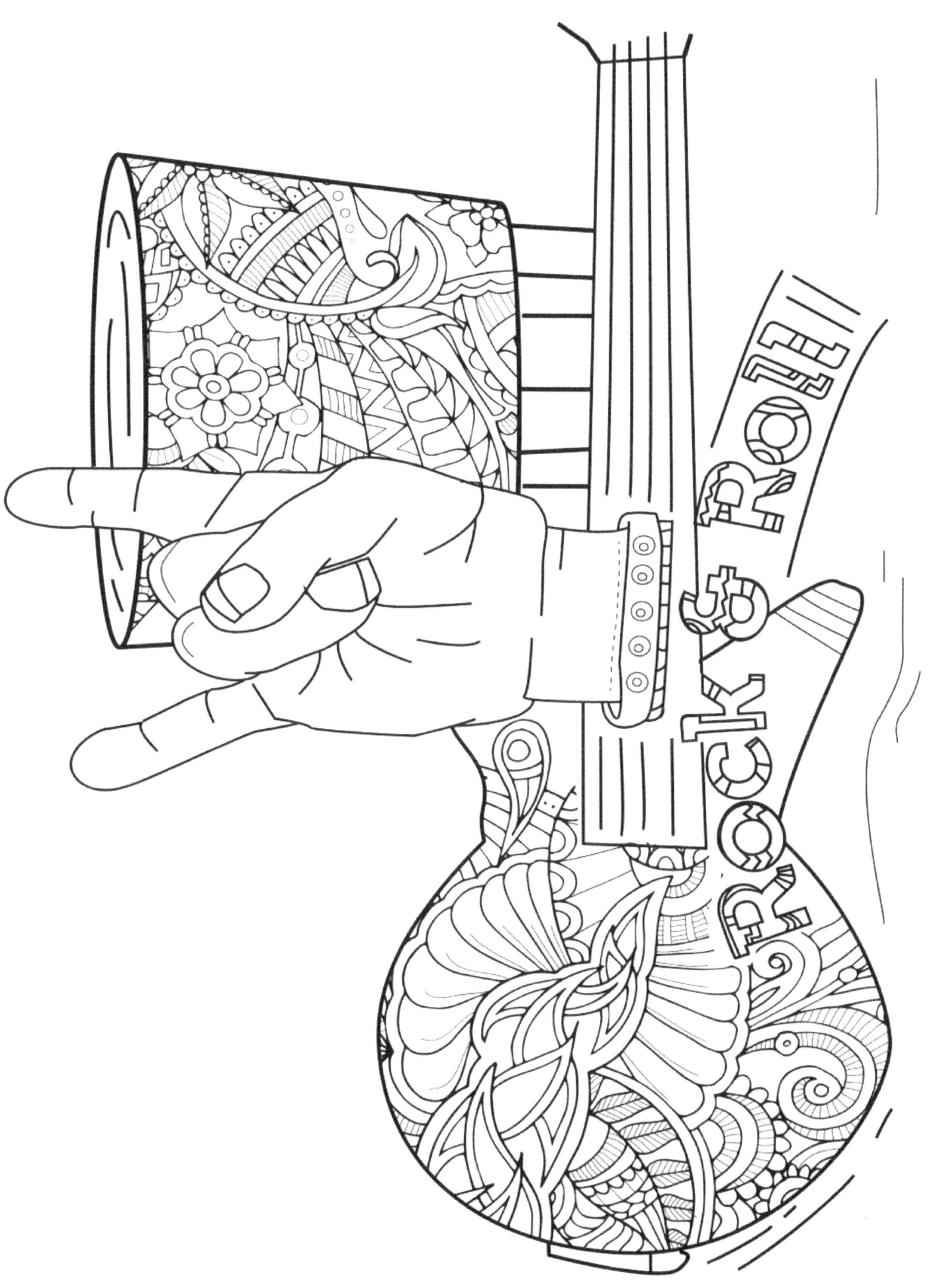

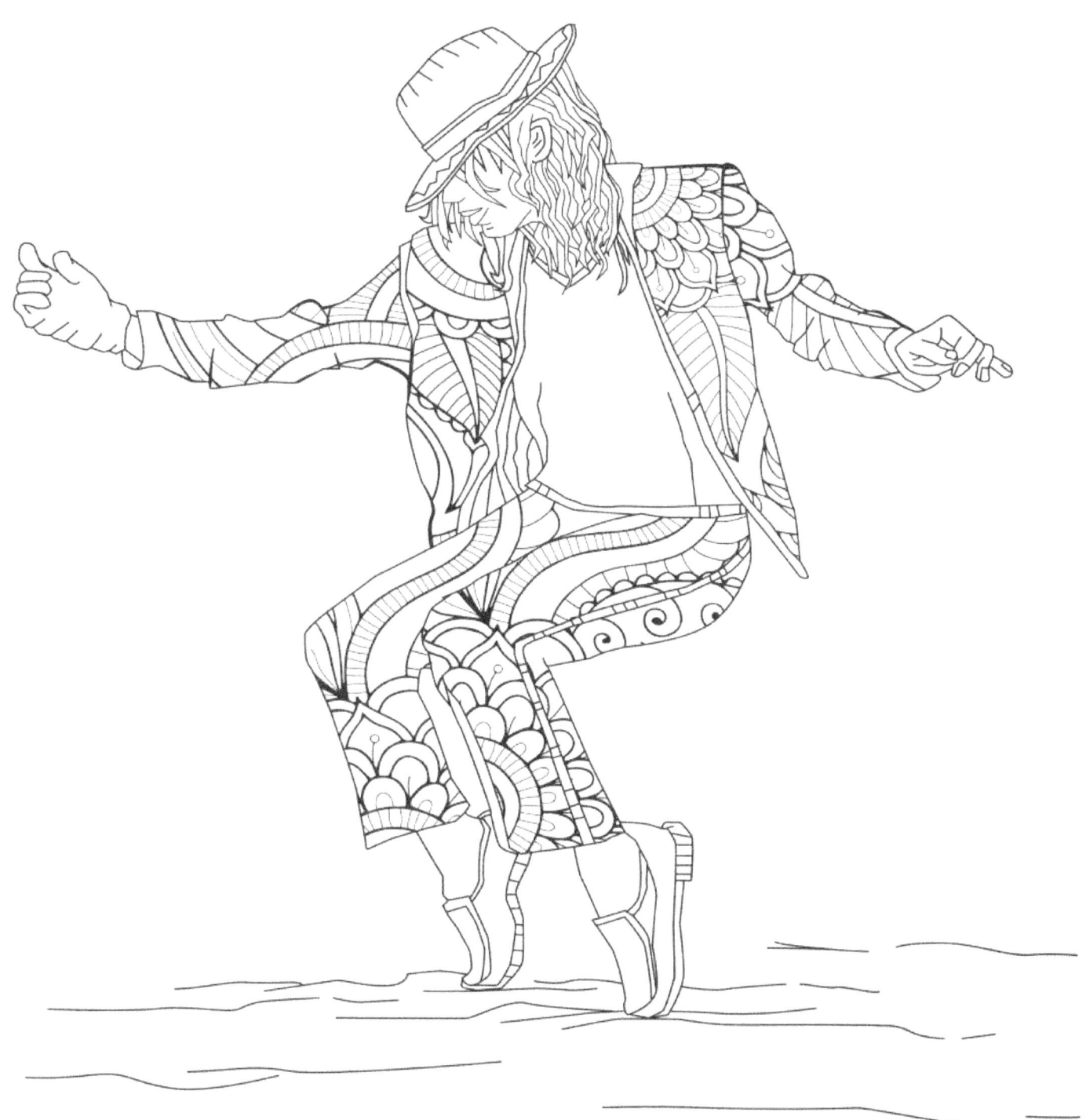

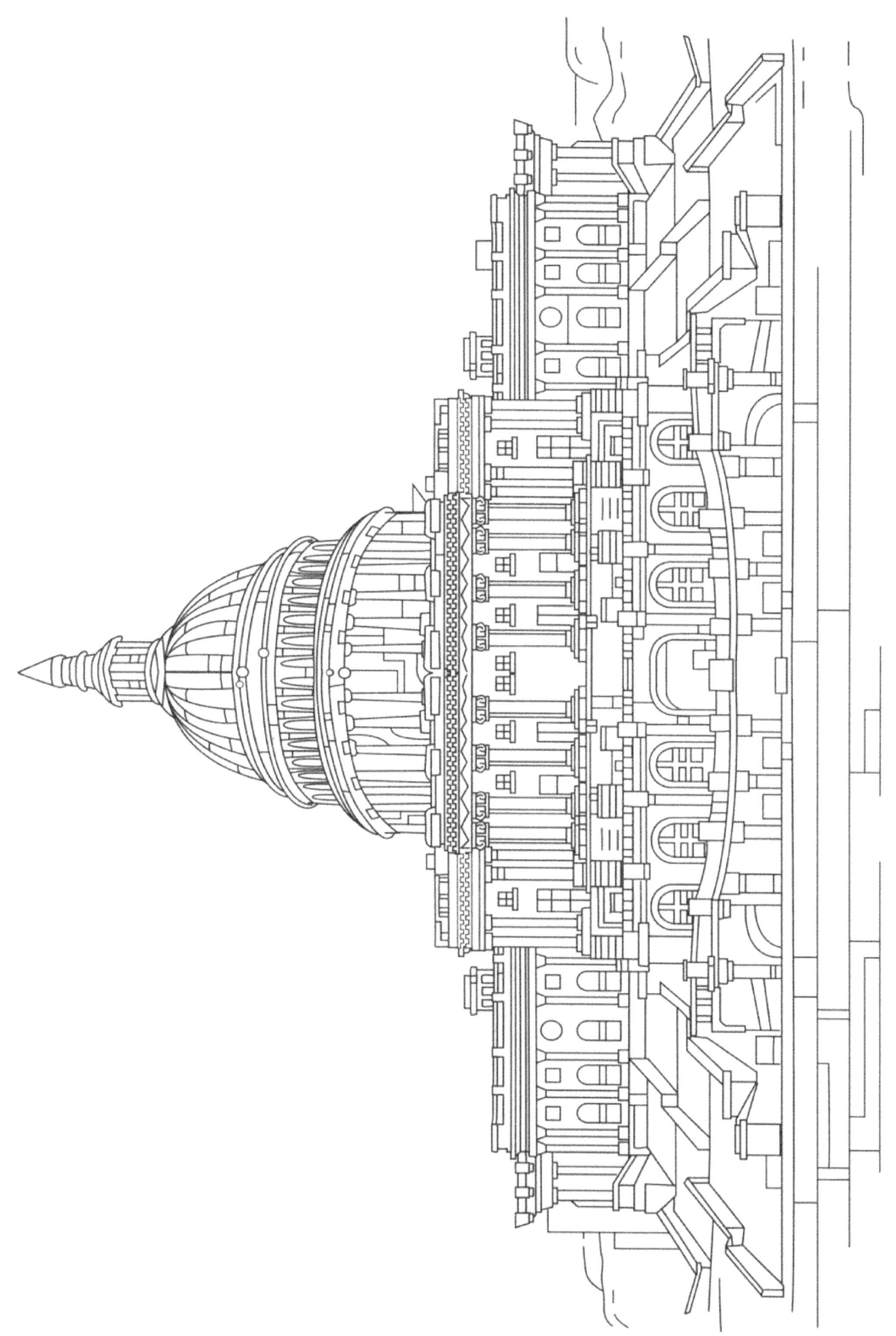

USA Facts

1. The United States of America became a country on the 4th July, 1776, when the declaration of Independence was signed. Every year Americans celebrate Independence Day on that date.

2. In 2017 there were almost 326 million people living in America.

3. The USA is divided into 50 states. The largest is Alaska, which was purchased from Russia in 1867, and the smallest is Rhode Island.

4. The most recent state to join America, in 1959, was Hawaii. It's also the furthest state away form the mainland.

5. The tallest mountain in mainland America is Mount Mckinley. It's 6,194 metres tall.

6. America's most inhabited city is New York, then Los Angeles and Chicago.

7. English is the most commonly spoken language in America, but there's a large number of Spanish speakers too.

8. America's most popular sports are American Football, Baseball, Basketball, and Ice Hockey.

9. The US consumes far more petrol than any other country in the world.

10. There are as many guns in private ownership in America as there are people, but only one in three people actually owns one.

11. The national animal of the USA is the Bald Eagle.

12. The currency used by America is the dollar. It's also referred to as the 'buck' or the 'greenback'.

13. The favourite food of Americans is the hamburger. This is followed closely by pizza, with over 100 acres of it being served every day.

14. The US flag has 50 stars on it to represent each of the states. It was designed by Robert G. Heft in 1958 when he was a high school student.

15. The capital city of the USA is Washington, DC. It was originally New York, though, between 1785 and 1790.

16. The United States has the largest economy in the world.

17. Columbus is said to have discovered the Americas in 1492 but, while his expedition led to the European colonisation of the region, there's evidence to suggest Norse settlers travelled there more than 400 years earlier.

18. The first President of America was George Washington. Since then there have been a further 44 men who have held the position.

19. The majority of the world's tornadoes occur in the US. More than 1,000 strike every year, most of which are in the states of Nebraska, South Dakota, Texas, Oklahoma, and Kansas.

20. The longest river system in the US is formed by the Mississippi and Missouri rivers. It's the fourth longest in the world.

USA Word Search

Can you find all of the hidden words?

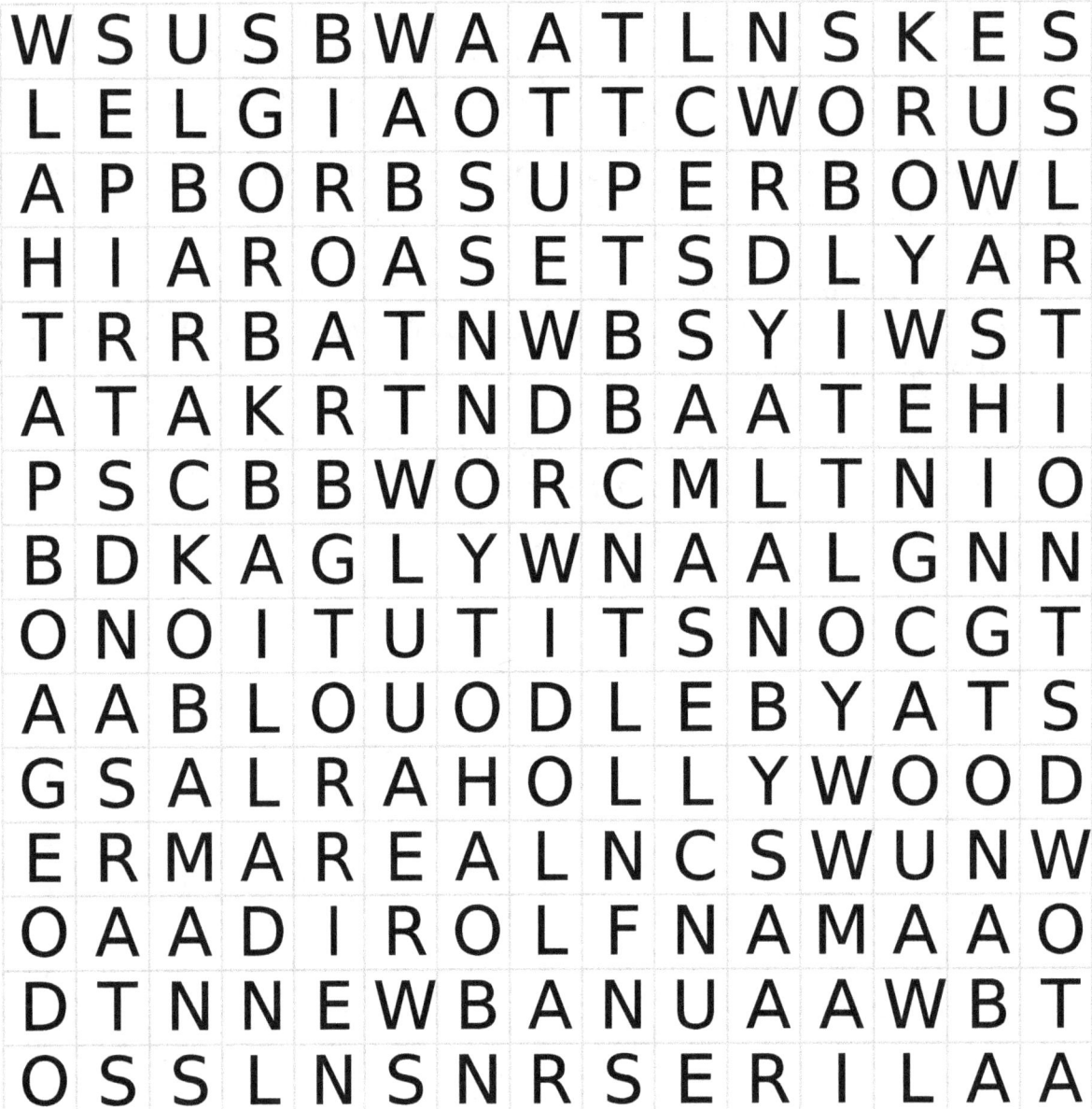

W	S	U	S	B	W	A	A	T	L	N	S	K	E	S
L	E	L	G	I	A	O	T	T	C	W	O	R	U	S
A	P	B	O	R	B	S	U	P	E	R	B	O	W	L
H	I	A	R	O	A	S	E	T	S	D	L	Y	A	R
T	R	R	B	A	T	N	W	B	S	Y	I	W	S	T
A	T	A	K	R	T	N	D	B	A	A	T	E	H	I
P	S	C	B	B	W	O	R	C	M	L	T	N	I	O
B	D	K	A	G	L	Y	W	N	A	A	L	G	N	N
O	N	O	I	T	U	T	I	T	S	N	O	C	G	T
A	A	B	L	O	U	O	D	L	E	B	Y	A	T	S
G	S	A	L	R	A	H	O	L	L	Y	W	O	O	D
E	R	M	A	R	E	A	L	N	C	S	W	U	N	W
O	A	A	D	I	R	O	L	F	N	A	M	A	A	O
D	T	N	N	E	W	B	A	N	U	A	A	W	B	T
O	S	S	L	N	S	N	R	S	E	R	I	L	A	A

Barack Obama	Florida	Stars and Stripes
Baseball	Grand Canyon	Superbowl
Constitution	Hollywood	Uncle Sam
Dollar	New York	Washington

USA Quiz

Questions

1. How many stars are there on the US flag?
2. What is the tallest mountain in mainland America?
3. On which date do Americans celebrate Independence Day?
4. What is the national bird of America?
5. Which city in America is home to the most people?
6. Most movie studios are based in which region of Los Angeles?
7. How many US Presidents have there been?
8. What is the nickname given to the region of America, which frequently sees tornadoes?
9. America was the country to first send a man to the moon in 1969. Who was the first to set foot on the surface?
10. Which popular sport is played at the Super bowl?
11. Which country lies to the North of 48 of the US states?
12. The US population is about 100 million people. TRUE or FALSE?
13. Which Marvel superhero, with an indestructible shield, was a patriotic super soldier who fought in the Second World War?
14. In which state would you expect to find a Disney them park and alligators?
15. Who is the current President of America?
16. Which American city has a basketball team whose nickname is the bulls?
17. How many international airports are there in New York?
18. What three colours are used on the US flag?
19. What is the State animal of California?
20. Which 5-sided building is home to the US defence forces?

Spot The Difference

6 Differences to Spot. Can You Spot Them All?

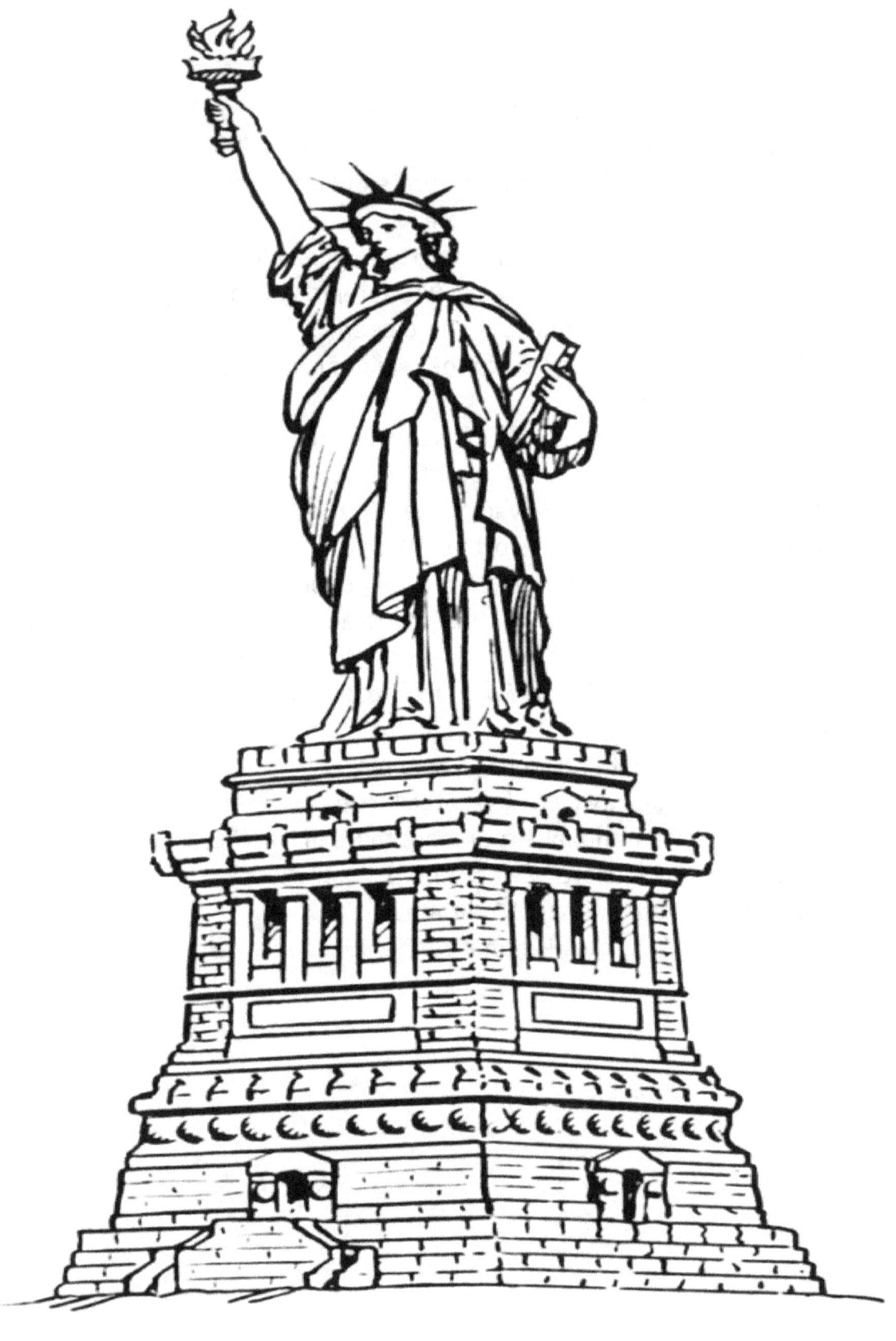

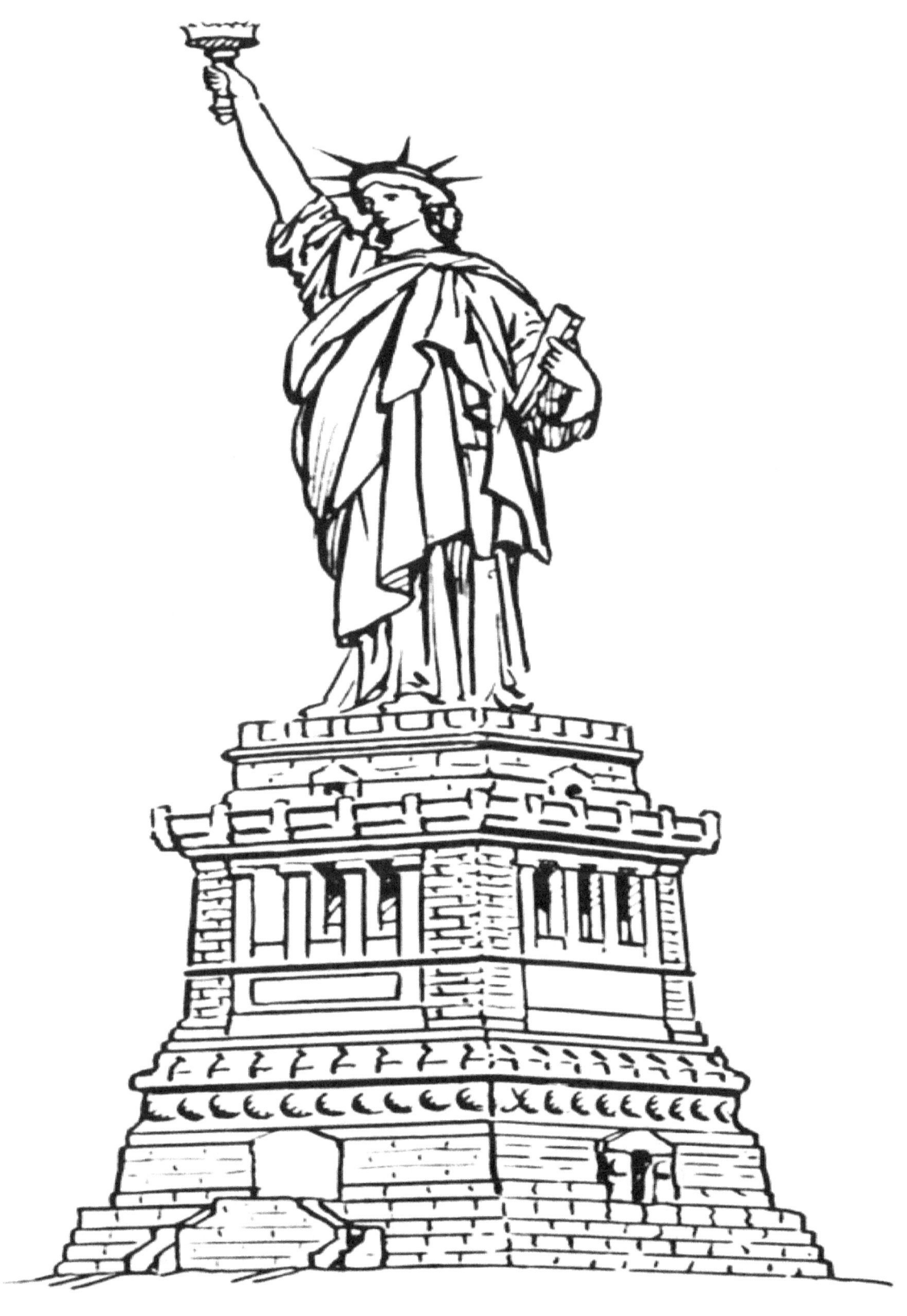

USA Crossword

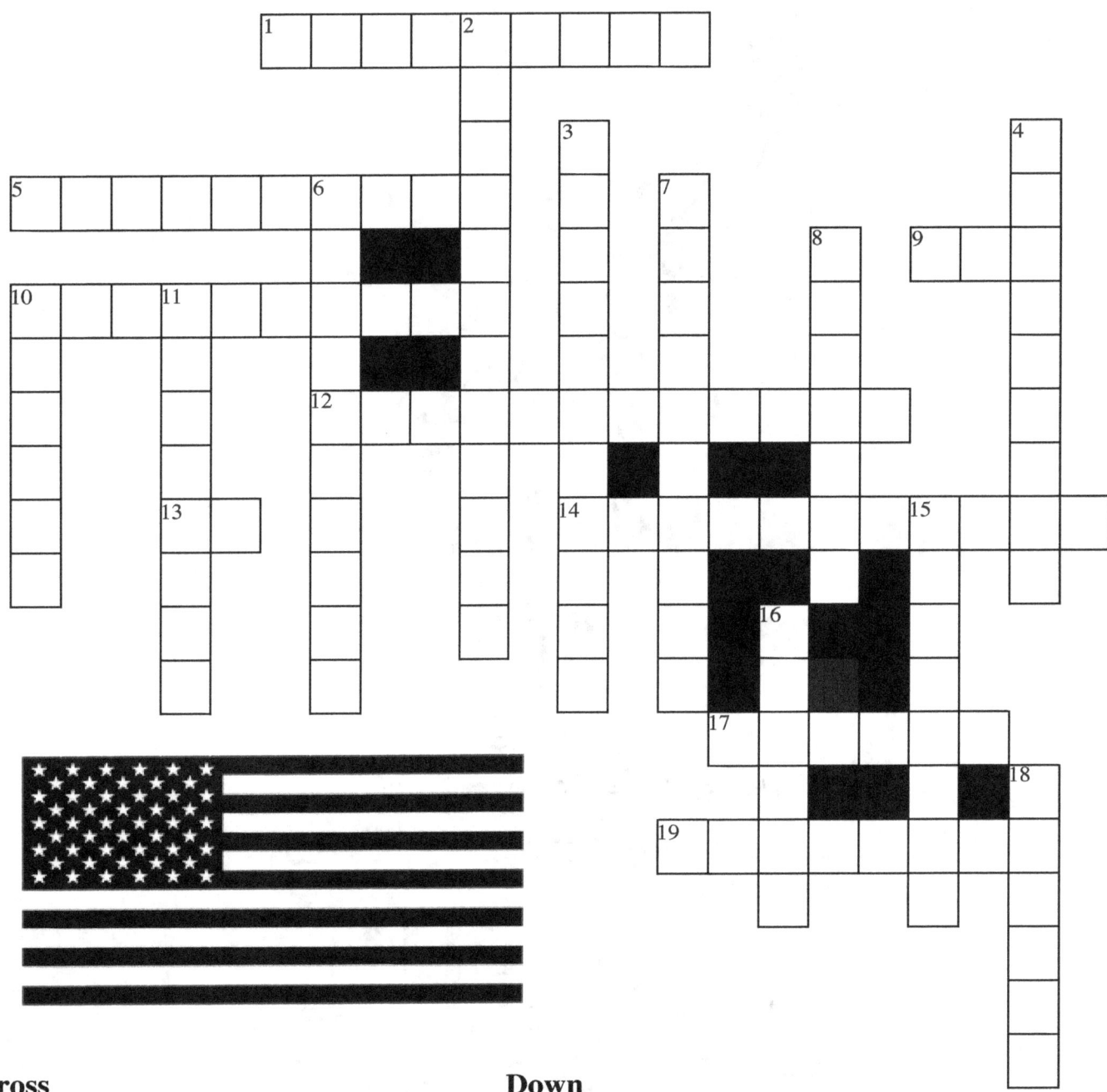

Across

1. The author of 'The Adventures of Huckleberry Finn' (4, 5)

5. The surname of America's first president (10)

9. Air Force ___, the name of the President's plane (3)

10. Most popular food in America (10)

12. The King of Rock and Roll (5, 7)

13. Washington _____, the Capital city of the USA (2)

14. The smallest US state (5, 6)

17. Biggest entertainment company in America (6)

19. Most popular sport in America (8)

Down

2. American holiday celebrated on the fourth Thursday of November (12)

3. Writer of the song 'I will always love you' (5, 6)

4. Name of the bus company that serves over 3,800 destinations (9)

6. The famous art museum in New York (10)

7. Where the President lives (5, 5)

8. The Capital City of Arizona (7)

10. American state that is furthest from California (6)

11. Main theatre street of New York (8)

15. City famed for gambling and being in a desert (3, 5)

16. Inventor of the mass market light bulb (6)

18. The largest US state (6)

USA Word Search

Can you find all of the hidden words?

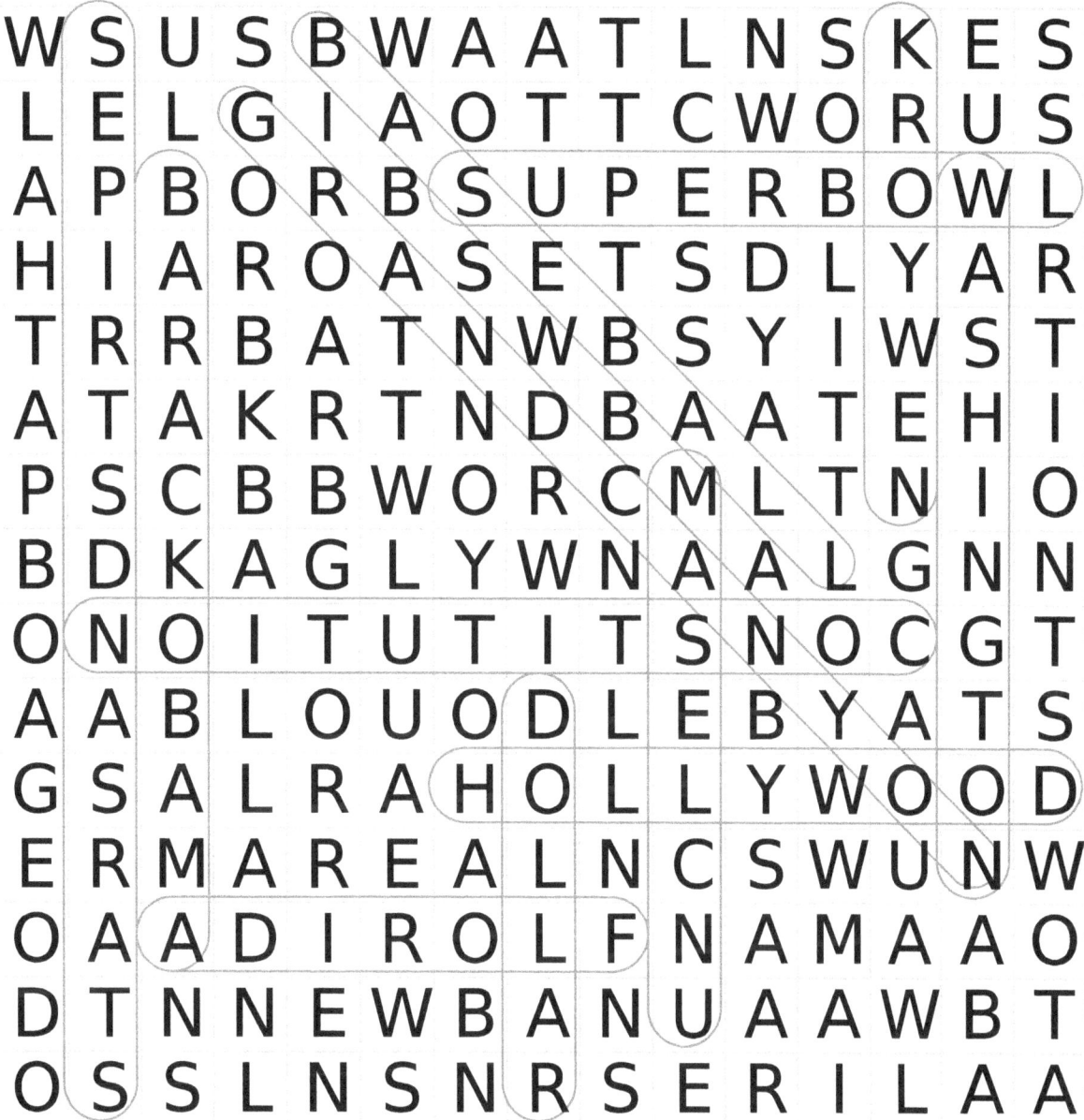

W	S	U	S	B	W	A	A	T	L	N	S	K	E	S
L	E	L	G	I	A	O	T	T	C	W	O	R	U	S
A	P	B	O	R	B	S	U	P	E	R	B	O	W	L
H	I	A	R	O	A	S	E	T	S	D	L	Y	A	R
T	R	R	B	A	T	N	W	B	S	Y	I	W	S	T
A	T	A	K	R	T	N	D	B	A	A	T	E	H	I
P	S	C	B	B	W	O	R	C	M	L	T	N	I	O
B	D	K	A	G	L	Y	W	N	A	A	L	G	N	N
O	N	O	I	T	U	T	I	T	S	N	O	C	G	T
A	A	B	L	O	U	O	D	L	E	B	Y	A	T	S
G	S	A	L	R	A	H	O	L	L	Y	W	O	O	D
E	R	M	A	R	E	A	L	N	C	S	W	U	N	W
O	A	A	D	I	R	O	L	F	N	A	M	A	A	O
D	T	N	N	E	W	B	A	N	U	A	A	W	B	T
O	S	S	L	N	S	N	R	S	E	R	I	L	A	A

Barack Obama
Baseball
Constitution
Dollar

Florida
Grand Canyon
Hollywood
New York

Stars and Stripes
Superbowl
Uncle Sam
Washington

Answers

1. 50
2. Mount Mckinley
3. 4th July
4. The Bald Eagle
5. New York
6. Hollywood
7. 45
8. Tornado Alley
9. Neil Armstrong
10. American Football
11. Canada
12. FALSE. It's actually 326 million people.
13. Captain America
14. Florida
15. Donald Trump
16. Chicago
17. Three. John F Kennedy, La Guardia, and Newark.
18. Red, White, and Blue
19. The Grizzly bear. (Even though none have been seen there since 1922)
20. The Pentagon

Spot The Difference

1. The flame of the torch
2. One of the rays of her crown
3. The rear part of her dress,
4. The furthest left window
5. The banner on the right
6. The door to the left

Thank you for purchasing this book.

If you would like to know more about Aryla Publishing Books please visit:-

www.ArylaPublishing.com

Or follow us on
Facebook
Twitter
Instagram
for *free promotions*

@arylapublishing

We would love to know what you think of this book so please leave us a review.

Have a wonderful day

Other Coloring Books from Aryla Publishing

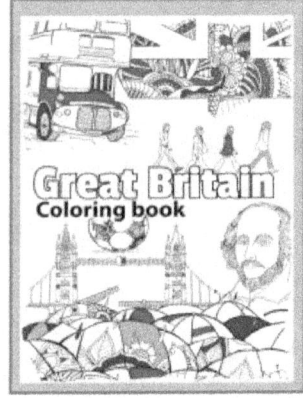
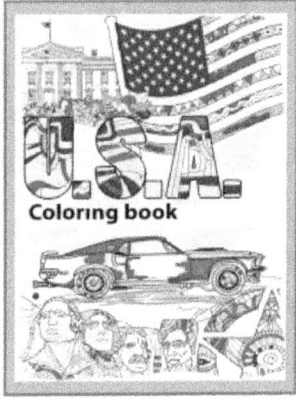
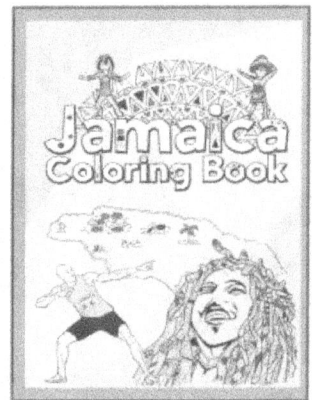
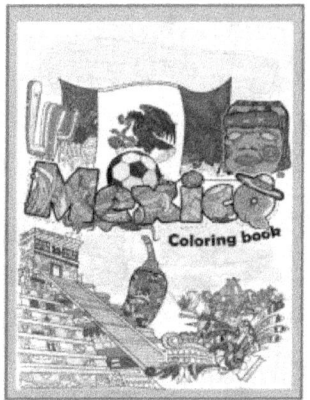

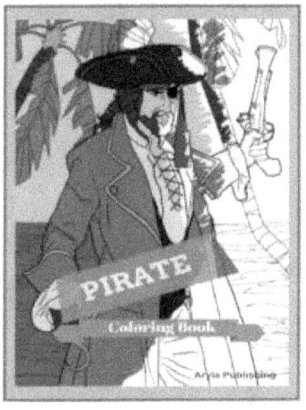
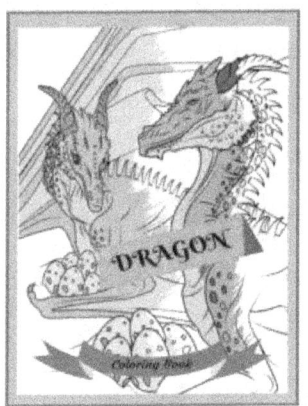
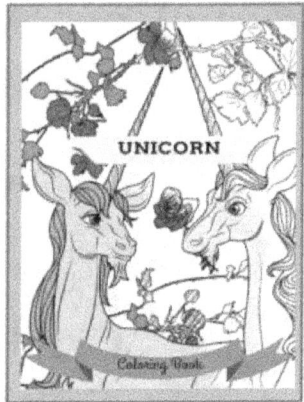
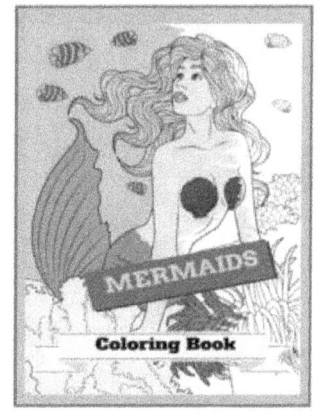

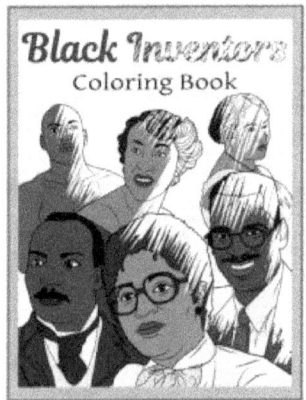
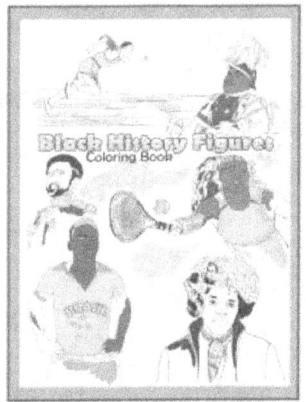
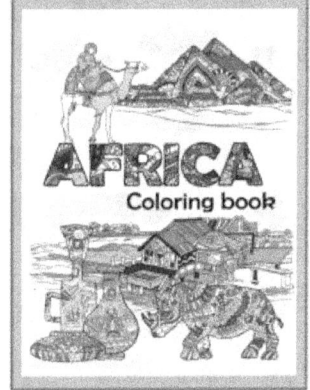
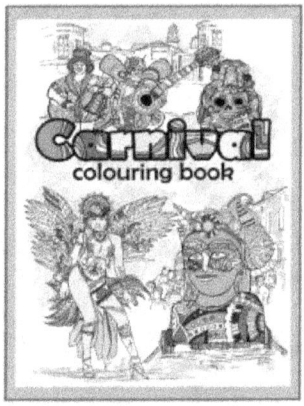

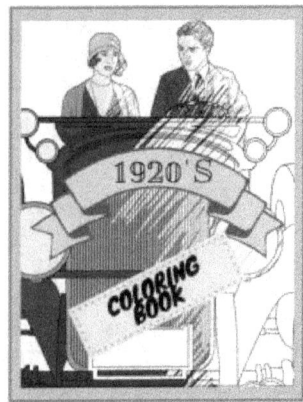
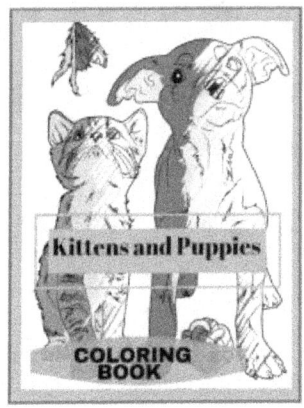
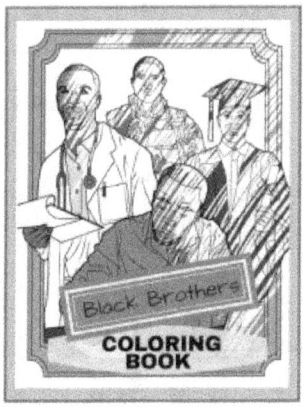
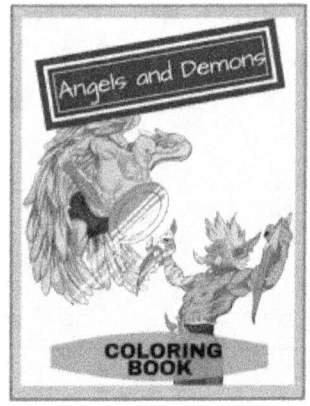

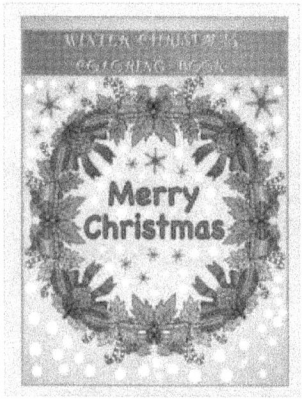
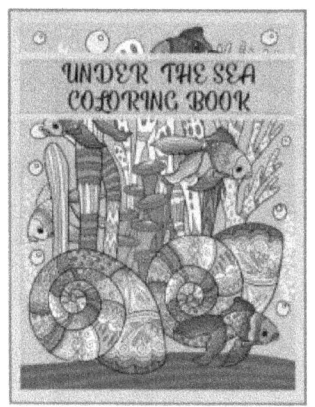
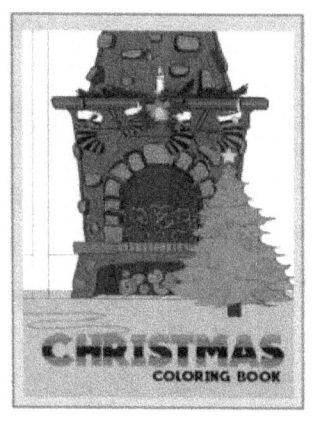
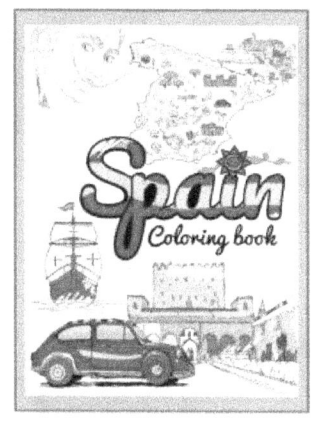
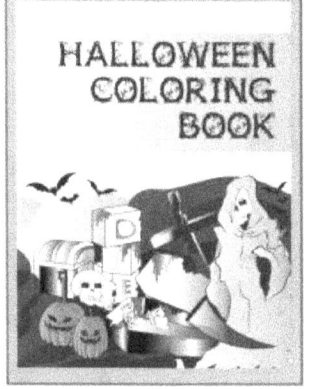
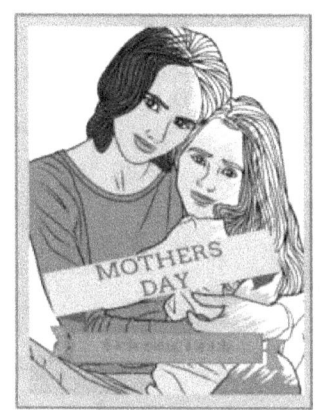
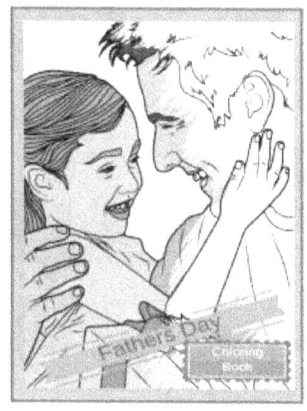
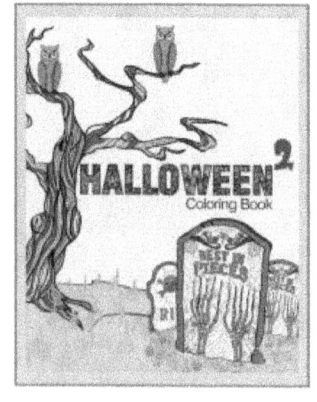
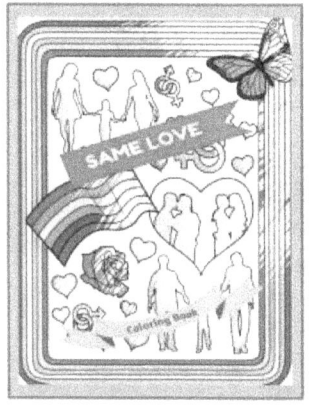
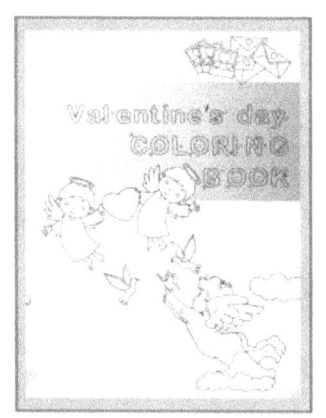
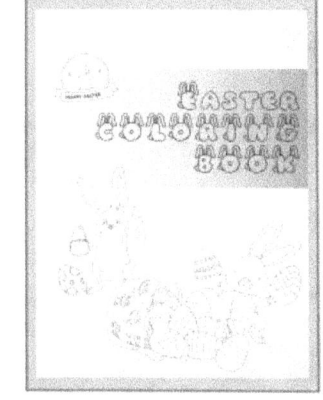
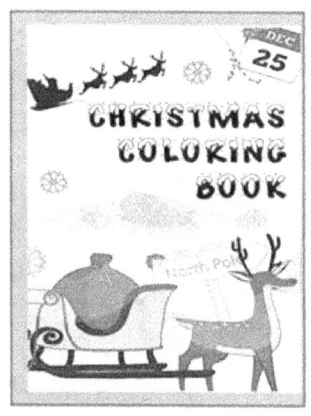
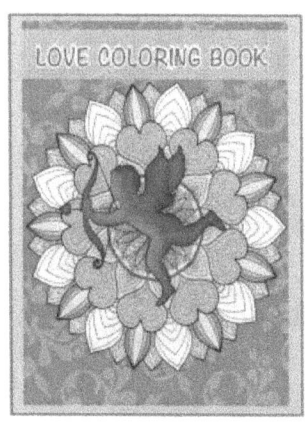
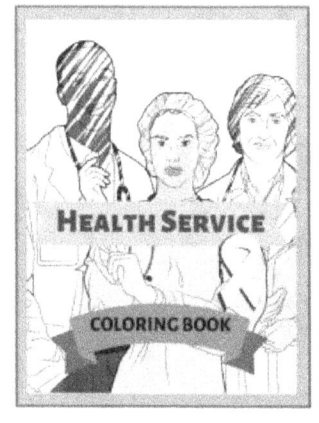
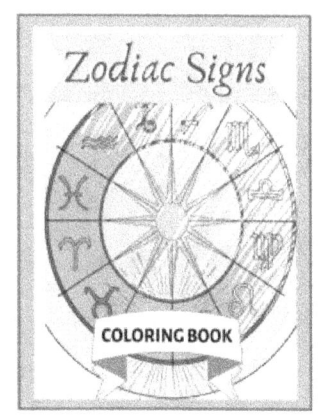
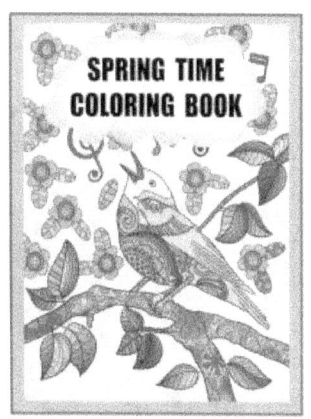

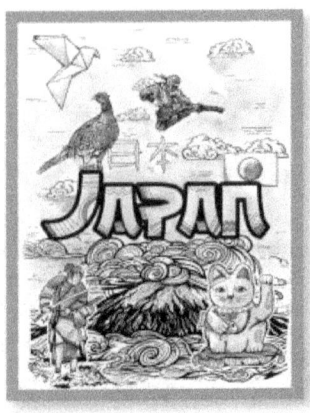

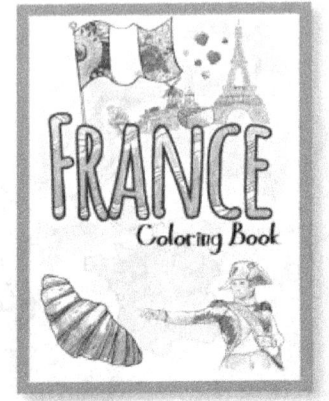

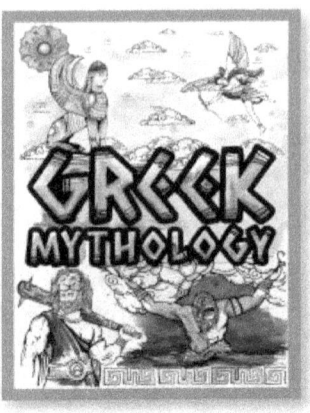

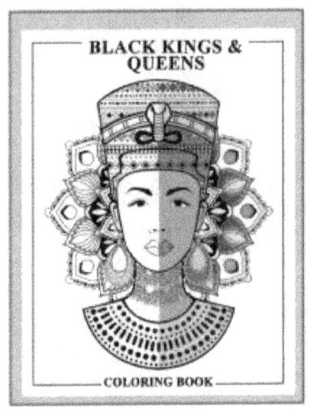

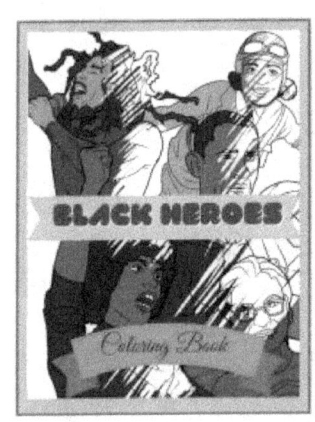

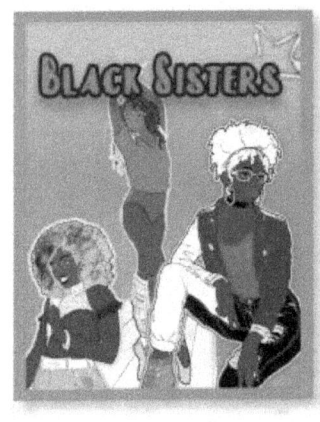

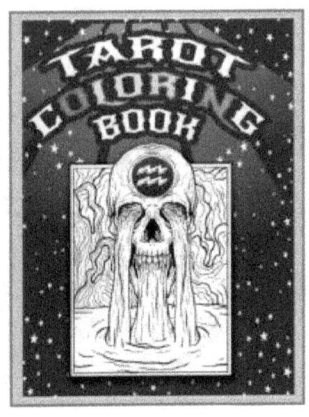

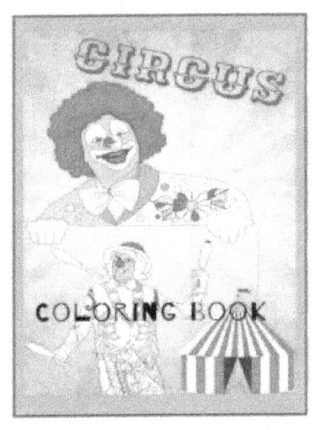

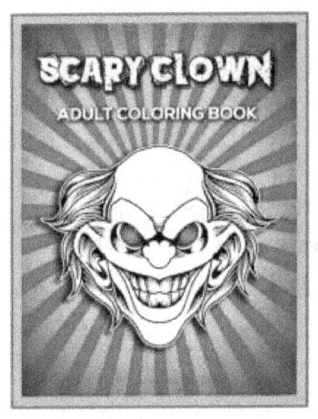

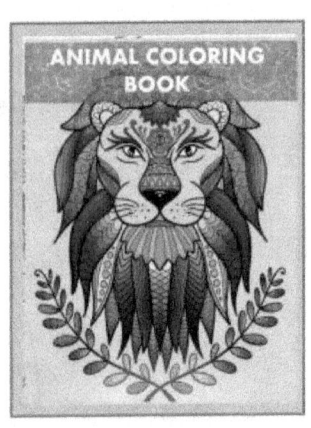

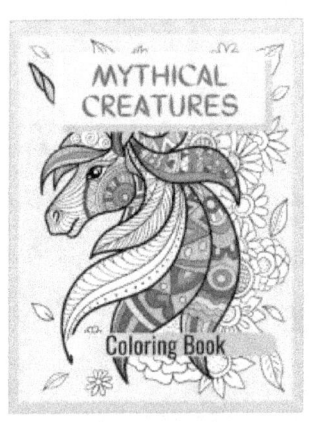

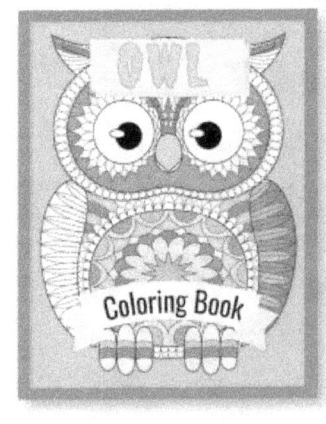

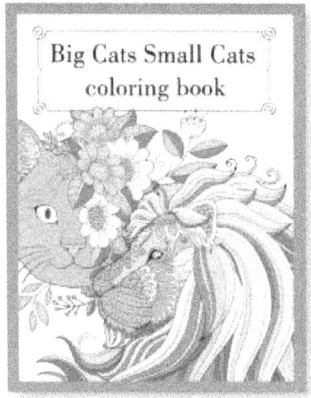

Big Cats Small Cats
coloring book

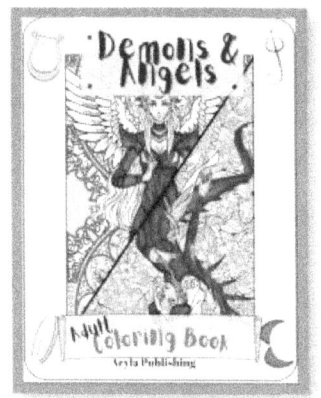

Demons & Angels

Myth Coloring Book
Aryla Publishing

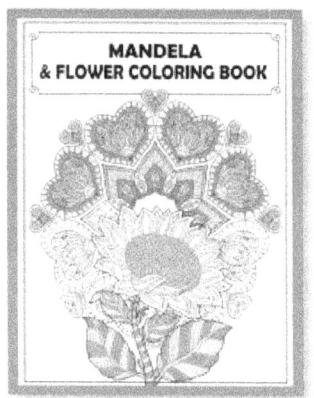

MANDELA
& FLOWER COLORING BOOK

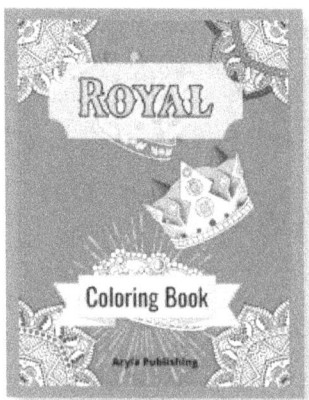

ROYAL

Coloring Book

Aryla Publishing

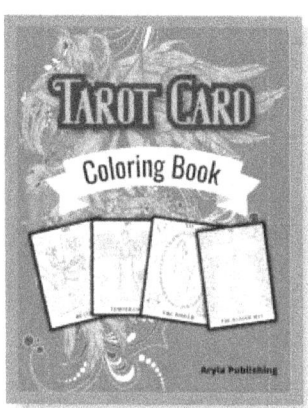

TAROT CARD

Coloring Book

Aryla Publishing

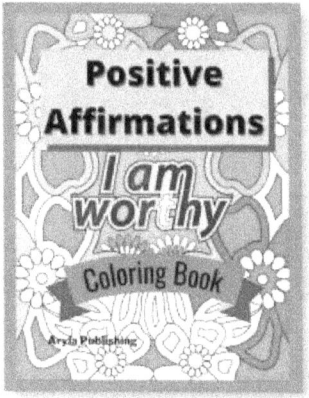

Positive
Affirmations
I am
worthy
Coloring Book

Aryla Publishing

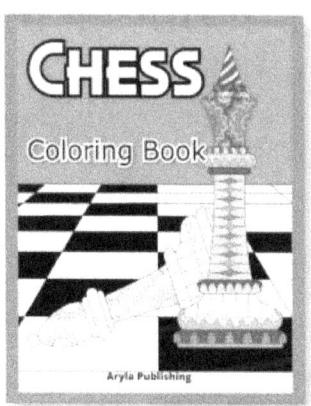

CHESS
Coloring Book

Aryla Publishing

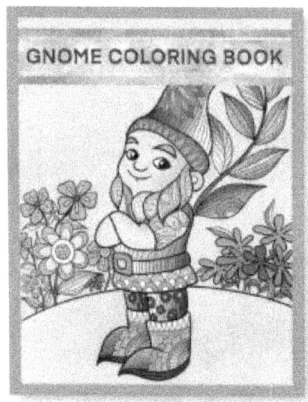

GNOME COLORING BOOK

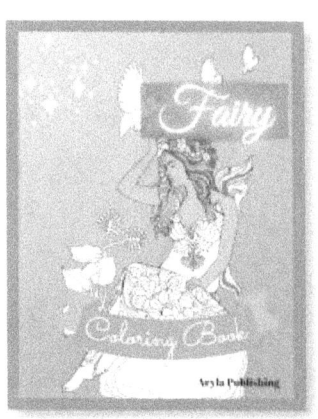

Fairy

Coloring Book

Aryla Publishing

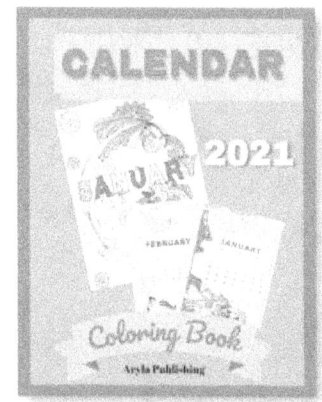

CALENDAR
2021

FEBRUARY   JANUARY

Coloring Book
Aryla Publishing

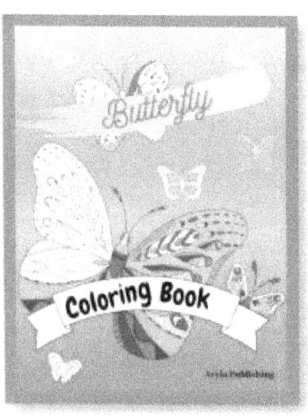

Butterfly

Coloring Book

Aryla Publishing

Visit **www.ArylaPublishing.com**
to find out about all new releases.

Follow us @arylapublishing on Twitter Instagram & Facebook

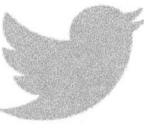  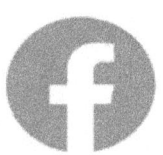

Search for Aryla Publishing on

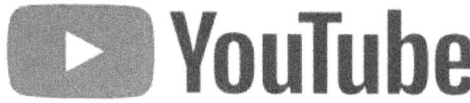 YouTube

Check out our <u>Book Trailers</u>

<u>Subscribe </u>to keep up to date with new releases!

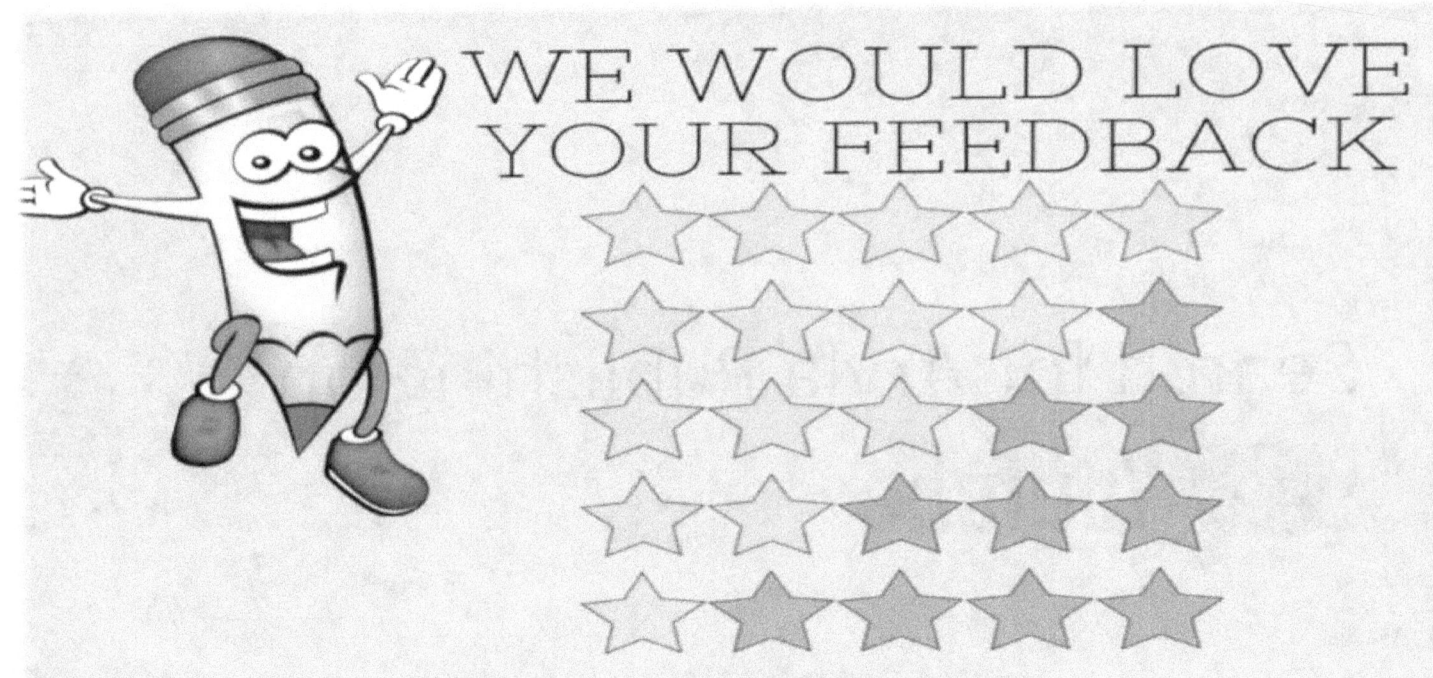

WE WOULD LOVE YOUR FEEDBACK

PLEASE LEAVE REVIEW AT:-

http://bit.ly/USAColorReview

Or use the QR code below